**"An interesting tool for working with gender differences."**
**—John Gray.**
**Author of *Men Are from Mars, Women Are from Venus***

"The more women have opportunities to play sports the more proficient they will become in competing in this men's world of 'unwritten rules.' To bridge the gap, Mendell's book, *How Men Think*, is a necessary guide for women working with men."
—Diane Everett, Ph.D.
Executive Director
National Association for Girls and Women in Sport

"Well-written, straightforward, and extremely honest and insightful . . . The culture of work is still controlled by men; ambitious women need to know how to avoid letting it defeat them."

—Pepper Schwartz
Author of *Love Between Equals*

Please turn the page for more rave reviews . . .

"Reading Mendell's exploration of the 'man's world' that prevails in business, sports, and war, we see a modern-day Margaret Mead hard at work studying a foreign culture. . . . Until this book, discussing gender differences in mixed company could generate as much hostility as the topics of sex, politics, and religion. . . . [But] *How Men Think* fosters a compassionate and even accepting attitude toward male attributes many women perceive as ridiculous foibles or even unforgivable sins. . . . [and] offers practical guidance for women working with men who have these attributes."

> —Alexandra Lajoux
> Editor
> *Director's Monthly*
> National Association of Corporate Directors

"Adrienne Mendell has succinctly captured the male-dominated business playing field and given us the tools to survive and to change the rules. . . . A clear, concise business primer for women who need to survive the 'old boys network' and who want to create a new work paradigm."

> —Geri Swift
> President
> Geri Swift Associates Management Consulting

# HOW MEN THINK

## The Seven Essential Rules for Making It in a Man's World

ADRIENNE MENDELL, M.A.

Fawcett Columbine / New York

A Fawcett Columbine Book
Published by Ballantine Books

http://www.randomhouse.com

Names and identifying characteristics of those interviewed for this publication have been altered or deleted. Any similarities with the names or characteristics of any living persons are purely coincidental and not intended by the author.

Grateful acknowledgment is made to *The Washington Post* for permission to reprint an excerpt from "Social Climate Changes but Finns Still Hot for Sauna" by Michael Dobbs, March 8, 1992 (as published in the *Philadelphia Inquirer*). Copyright © 1992 *The Washington Post*. Reprinted with permission.

Library of Congress Cataloging-in-Publication Data
Mendell, Adrienne.
    How men think : the seven essential rules for making it in a man's world /
Adrienne Mendell.—1st ed.
       p.   cm.
    ISBN 0-449-90978-6
    1. Women—Employment—Psychological aspects.   2. Sex role in the
work environment.   3. Men—Psychology.   I. Title.
HD6053.M45   1996
650.1'082—dc20                                                    95-54010

Cover design by Barbara Leff
Text design by Mary A. Wirth

Manufactured in the United States of America
First Edition: April 1996
10  9  8  7  6  5  4  3  2  1

Jana—

Welcome to adulthood! Unfortunately it's a man's adulthood out in the "real world." I hope you get some useful tips from this book that will help you succeed in this cruel "man's world."

Happy 18th Birthday

I love you

Dad

5/2/98

# CONTENTS

# ACKNOWLEDGMENTS

There are so many people who had a hand in helping me create this book that it is impossible to thank them all individually. So first I would like to extend a general thank-you to all the people that have touched my life and contributed to this book in many different ways.

I would like to thank the men and women who were kind enough to let me interview them for this book, the many women in my groups who shared their stories, the friends who spoke with me informally about gender issues, and the skippers and crew who sailed with me and shared their knowledge and wisdom.

I would also like to thank my agent, Jane Dystel, and my editors, Sherri Rifkin and Elizabeth Zack, who helped me turn my early attempts at a manuscript into a polished book.

You know you have good friends when they agree to read your rough drafts. Roberta Galati, Pricilla Rosenwald, and Terri Smith read parts of the early drafts and cheered me on. Joanne Buzzetta, Roberta Galati, Judy Kornfeld, Terri Smith, and Susan Swenk were always willing to brainstorm with me, listen when I needed to talk, and provide the kind of support only good friends can give.

The Philadelphia Women's Network and the Professional Women's Lunch Group were invaluable in boosting my spirits and confidence when times were rough.

I owe a very special debt of gratitude to Terri Smith, who was willing to play the out-of-character role of nag. Whenever I needed it, she contributed world-class badgering to make sure I stopped sailing long enough to meet my deadlines.

I especially want to thank and acknowledge Joan Saltzman. Joan began this research with me and helped me turn a vague idea into a working hypothesis. Her clarity of thinking and organizational abilities remain a model for me.

# HOW
# MEN
# THINK

# PART ONE

# HOW THE GAME BEGAN

# Introduction

Nineteen years ago, a friend and I decided to follow one of our dreams. We went off to the Annapolis Sailing School for a weekend course. I fell in love with sailing instantly. The grace of the boats, the feel of the wind, and the sound of the water moving past the hull all gave me a sense of contentment that I hadn't expected. I knew I had to make this sport part of my life. I wanted to become the best sailor I could, and learning to race seemed the most direct way to achieve that goal. I began racing, and at that time I was one of very few women racing on the Chesapeake Bay and almost always the only woman skipper at the regattas I attended. That hasn't changed very much. There are more women involved in racing now, but still few of them at the helm.

I had no idea of the profound changes competing in this sport would require of me. It had never occurred to me that all my competitors would be male. By the time I realized this, I was in the thick of it, and much too committed to racing to care.

When I first declared my intention to race, one of the racers laughingly said to me, "So you think you know how to make a sailboat go. Wait until you try to make a sailboat go fast." I didn't know what he meant.

Now I understand why he laughed. Racing is very demanding. I threw myself into it. I read every book I could find about racing. I went to sailboat racing clinics. But when I got out on the racecourse, I just couldn't translate what I had learned into action. I thought I knew a lot. I could quote the books; I knew sail trim, strategy, and all the rules. But it was clear that something else, something I couldn't put my finger on, was happening. The other racers' behavior and responses just didn't make sense to me. Worse yet, the other skippers didn't like me and clearly didn't want me around. I felt angry, resentful, and confused. The answer to all this came unexpectedly.

One day, in an attempt to be friendly, I made a joking comment to another crew about a mistake they had made the day before. I will never forget the response. An angry, frightening, low-pitched male growl arose from the boat, and they abruptly tacked away without a word. "What did I do wrong?" I cried out, astonished. To my further astonishment, a male crewmember proceeded to tell me.

I had heard other people teasing this crew about their mistake and thought I was doing the same thing. But what I had failed to notice was that the teasing had stopped after the party that followed that race. He didn't use these words, but in essence this crewmember told me there was an unwritten set of rules that everyone played by. Not only did I seem to be ignoring these rules, I was breaking them as well. I had just violated the unwritten rule that puts a time limit on teasing.

He told me that he knew I was a nice person off the water, but had been surprised and dismayed by my appalling behavior at the helm. He was glad to have an opportunity to speak up. Luckily my curiosity overrode my defensiveness and I began to ask questions. He was shocked by what I didn't know, and I was flabbergasted by what he was telling me.

I decided to use my skills as a psychologist to learn the rest of these unwritten rules. I asked endless questions of the men I was sailing with, and they answered readily. I observed the way the men interacted with each other and with me. I copied and experimented with the behaviors I observed. Eventually, I figured the puzzle out. I began to play by these unwritten rules. I became a much better racer and I started to have much more fun. Most surprising of all, the other skippers began to like, accept, and even respect me.

I am a psychotherapist by profession. My practice is in the center of Philadelphia and consists primarily of business and professional women and men. My training as a psychologist taught me to look for the source of my patients' problems within each person's psyche, but I was hearing too many of the same problems to consider them to be unique or isolated instances. If I were to assume that these problems originated within each person's psyche, I would have to believe that all the professional women in Philadelphia were suffering from a mass psychosis. I decided to look for an alternative explanation.

Curiously, I began to realize that the problems these women were having in their jobs were similar to the problems I had encountered racing my sailboat. I wondered if the same set of unwritten rules that were operative in sailboat racing were operative in business. Could these women's problems be a consequence of their ignorance of the unwritten rules of the game?

I felt frustrated seeing so many women suffering. Eventually, I called Joan Saltzman, an attorney and a friend, and said, "There have been too many professional women crying in my office. We have to do something." We met for lunch the next day and began brainstorming.

Joan and I systematically approached the task of learning how men think about work. First, we had to identify the problems women were having in their jobs. Then we studied the way men approach the workplace. Because Joan is a lawyer, we took advantage of her experiences and studied lawyers first. Since then, I have gone on to study other businesses and professions.

I used a variety of techniques to pinpoint the most common and most pressing problems for women. I listened to the patients in my psychotherapy practice and to my friends. I examined my own experiences. I ran problem-solving groups specifically for women with problems in the workplace. Joan and I ran focus groups of female lawyers to explore the problems they faced. Then I ran similar focus groups for business and professional women. It became clear that there was a consistent set of problems that crossed all parts of the workplace. These are the problems I will address in this book.

The next task was to learn how the workplace looks through a man's eyes. I had learned the unwritten rules of sailboat racing by asking the men, so I tried the same strategy in business. Joan and I began to identify and interview very successful lawyers. I added doctors, accountants, engineers, insurance executives, stockbrokers, business owners, etc. I tried to make my base as varied as possible. I formally interviewed over one hundred very successful men and spoke informally with countless others. For comparison and new insights, I also interviewed twenty very successful women.

All my male friends were fair game. Whenever I had a chance, I talked to them about the way they approached their work. I found most men to be fascinated and flattered by the fact that I was studying them. I was surprised at how willingly and how candidly they spoke to me. I taped and took notes during the formal interviews and learned to slip away unobtrusively to write down an especially juicy quote or a new idea during informal conversations.

For the formal interviews, I had no trouble getting subjects. The men I approached were delighted to be included in a study of very successful men. Each interview was unique, but I always managed to weave in a standard set of questions. I asked these men to describe how they approached their work, what they thought of their female colleagues, and what they thought women did best and worst. I asked them to describe the very best and very worst female coworker they had ever encountered, and how they thought women should change professionally.

My questioning verified something these men always knew to be true: women were "a problem" in business. I used my clinical skills to direct the conversation from general complaining to specifically defining these "problems." They were especially glad to help me find solutions because these men were frustrated with many of their female colleagues. In their eyes, women displayed consistently "inappropriate" behavior that puzzled them. The men felt they kept encountering unwarranted hostility from women and were at a loss as to how to respond to it. The men I interviewed seemed to be waiting for an opportunity to talk frankly, especially to a woman.

Their responses were too consistent across interviews not to be true. And not only were these men willing to talk about their approach to work, but they were also willing to describe tactics they use specifically against women in business situations. They were more than delighted to help me pinpoint what they considered women's self-defeating behaviors. Interestingly, the very successful women I interviewed shared many of the perceptions of the men.

The results of these interviews revealed a common theme that I think of as "the rules of the game of work." Men approach the workplace as if it were a battlefield or a sports contest. They approach their work with the same mind-set they use in competitive sports. Competitive sports, war, and the workplace are governed by a set of unwritten rules familiar to most men but unknown to most women.

In order to be competitive in the game of "work," it is necessary to learn the rules of the game. The men taught me the rules, and through this book I will teach them to you.

My goal in writing this book is not only to teach you the rules of the game, but to provide you with the knowledge and skills necessary to improve the quality of your life, reduce conflict and stress, and help you become as successful as you want to be. I don't like all of the rules that I describe, but right now these are the rules by which business plays. I hope this book will help women become successful and powerful enough to rewrite the rules.

Understanding gender differences is an essential skill for everyone in the workplace. When men and women understand their differences, behavior that was previously confusing begins to make sense. The more you know about the men with whom you work, the more comfortable and successful you will be. To really understand how men think and act, you have to learn how and why these behaviors developed. When you know why men act the way they do, their behavior becomes understandable and predictable.

Chapter One is an overview of the fundamental ways men and women differ—the biological, psychological, and cultural underpinnings of gender differences. It explores similarities and differences between men and women across time and across cultures.

Chapter Two explains the importance games play in male and female development. Girls and boys play dramatically different games. The very different games each sex plays teach very different skills and ways of interacting. The rules and philosophies men learn at play become the mores of the workplace. In Chapter Three, you'll discover that the problems women encounter in the workplace are remarkably similar to the problems four-year-old girls face in the playground. With this new insight, you will view male-female interaction from a new perspective.

The second part of this book is a detailed account of the rules of the game of "work." In business, as in any game, all players are expected to know the rules and to try their best to win. The first three chapters explain the advantages of viewing business as a game and describe the general structure of the game. Chapters Four to Ten are devoted to detailing the rules of the game. I'll describe the rules, illustrate them with vignettes, and give you practical advice on how to apply them.

Sometimes we can be our own worst enemy. I asked the men I interviewed to describe the worst woman with whom they had ever worked. They readily obliged. Their answers were remarkably consistent. The behaviors they talked about most were inability to deal comfortably with mistakes, passivity, and problems in setting priorities. These self-defeating behaviors are not unique to women, but they are more common in women than in men. In the third section, Chapters Eleven to Thirteen, I show you how to find out if these behaviors are a problem for you and how to change them if they are. These chapters include self-tests to help you identify these problems and contain step-by-step instructions on how to overcome them.

I also asked the men I interviewed about the strategies they used against adversaries—a colleague competing for the same job, or an opponent on the other side of a negotiation. They described techniques they used against both men and women, but I asked them to elaborate on the strategies they felt were especially effective against women. I devote the fourth part of this book, Chapters Fourteen to Eighteen, to describing these strategies in detail and giving you concrete ideas about how to combat them.

In Chapter Nineteen I'll take stock of where we were, where we are, and where we can go.

Trying to understand the causes and find solutions to the problems women encounter in the workplace has become an ongoing process for me. I have continued to interview successful men. I give speeches, run workshops, facilitate groups, and use this information in my psychotherapy practice. Learning how men think is enormously helpful to the women with whom I work.

Writing this book has been an extraordinary experience for me. I have learned about the way the world works, found new strengths in myself, and met some remarkable people. I hope reading this book can help you in similar ways. I hope it helps you earn the respect and rewards you deserve in the workplace.

# Boys Will Be Boys

*What do men want?*
—ANONYMOUS

It's a question we've all pondered—and especially women in the workplace. Here's what today's female professionals are experiencing:

NATALIE:

> When I made an excellent suggestion at the board meeting, it was greeted with silence. A few minutes later, a colleague of mine, Arthur, said the same thing. My boss promptly congratulated him for his original idea. Why do men ignore women?

CELESTE:

> I was pleased with the assertive way I handled the problem. But then I heard Will say to Joe, "Stay away from her today. She must have PMS." Why won't Will take me seriously?

HELEN:

> It was a brutal negotiation. Sam, our opponent; Joe, my partner; and I really fought it out. As I was packing up to

leave, Sam and Joe walked out together, laughing, leaving me behind. How could they be so friendly after being so tough on each other? And why did they leave me out?

DORIS:

The company denied my request for a promotion. My supervisor said that my skills weren't good enough, and added that I'm abrasive, aggressive, and have poor people skills. Men with less skill, who are downright rude and more aggressive than I will ever be, are routinely promoted. What can I do when faced with this type of discrimination?

CYNTHIA:

My presentation was excellent. I was sure I had won the account. But when the client smiled and said, "Thank you, sweetheart," I knew I didn't have a chance. How do you handle a man like that?

Why do so many competent women fail to get ahead? Why are so many men unsupportive, even hostile, to women in the workplace? Why do we have so many difficulties communicating with, and understanding, each other? How did we get so far apart in the first place!

It's necessary to go back to the beginning, because that's where all the difficulties in the workplace stem from.

In our society men and women are raised so differently that it is as if we grow up in two different worlds. Almost from birth, our experiences are so divergent that we can be standing side by side viewing the same event, yet come away with totally different impressions of what just happened. It is not an exaggeration to say that men and women live in separate realities.

Psychologists, psychiatrists, sociologists, anthropologists, and biologists all study human development. Experts in these fields may disagree about how and why men and women differ, but they all agree that gender differences exist. They disagree about how much of this difference is a result of nature and how much of nurture, but they universally agree that children are affected by both. Understanding how and why gender differences develop is crucial. With this knowledge, behavior and attitudes that seemed inexplicable now make sense. Rather than feeling bewildered and frustrated when working with men, you can use this information to learn how to problem-solve effectively.

## Our Basic Equipment

It is impossible to understand male-female differences without considering the biological aspects. Clearly men and women are physically different in size, body shape, strength, and hormonal makeup. It is hardly surprising that these differences have an influence on behavior.

Biological differences between males and females begin at conception and are enhanced during gestation. At conception, the only physical difference between male and female embryos is that female embryos have two X chromosomes while male embryos have an X and a Y chromosome. For the first six weeks of gestation male and female embryos develop identically. To be precise, for the first six weeks all embryos are physiologically female. During the sixth week, the Y chromosome in the male goes to work and causes the fetus to produce a hormone called testosterone.

Testosterone is the male hormone. Without it, all babies would be born female. The presence of testosterone in the uterus causes the fetus to change and develop male physical characteristics. The effect of testosterone is so powerful that if an embryo that is genetically female (has two X chromosomes) is exposed to testosterone, it will develop all the secondary sexual characteristics of a male.

After birth, most testosterone is created by the testes, but a small amount of it is also secreted by the adrenal gland. Only men have testes, but both men and women have adrenal glands, and so both produce testosterone. The amount produced varies from person to person, but men produce much more than women.

Levels of testosterone have been linked to aggression in both males and females.[1] Men who have more testosterone than average are more aggressive than the average male. Women who have more testosterone than average are more aggressive than the average female. Because men have so much more testosterone in their bodies than women, many scientists believe that men have a biological predisposition toward aggression.

In all animals, including humans, physical instincts affect behavior. But in humans, socialization, culture, and the ability to think mediate this influence. Most of the time, socialization overrules physical instincts, but the remnants of these physical instincts still exist. For example, sexual attraction seems to be related to unseen molecules called pheromones. This means that, at least to a small extent, we are attracted to a particular person because we like the way he or she smells. Similarly, our sleeping patterns are dictated by our hormones. Hormone levels and body temperature ebb and flow in a cycle of approximately twenty-four hours. We all have a natural pattern of sleeping and waking, determined by our bodies. This varies from person to person, with some people preferring to be up early in the morning, and others preferring to rise late and stay up late. But regardless of our innate pattern, our socialization overrides it and we work whatever hours our schedules require.

## Echoes of the Caveman

Darwin's concept of "survival of the fittest" provides an explanation of why aggression would be universally encouraged in men and nurturance universally encouraged in women. Survival of the fittest means that nature dictates that animals with traits that help perpetuate the species survive. Animals without these traits die off. These traits are passed on from generation to generation. Consider the traits that have been passed down from generation to generation in humans.

In Darwinian terms, females have developed and passed on the special traits needed to bear and care for infants. Males have developed and passed on the special traits needed to ensure the survival of the childbearer. Bearing children makes females physically vulnerable and in need of protection part of the time. The job of protector goes to the sex that does not get pregnant: males. To be successful protectors, males have to be physically strong and primed to fight when necessary. To ensure survival of the infants, females have to be nurturing.

Too much nurturance in a caveman might hinder his ability to fight when necessary. Too much aggression in women might mean too few pregnant women. These two traits, aggression in the male and nurturance in the female, helped propagate the species. For untold centuries, this specialization of the sexes made sense.

## Around the World

In her book *Feminism and Psychoanalytic Theory*,[2] Dr. Nancy Chodorow summarizes the cross-cultural differences between men and women. There are no personality traits that exist *only* in men or *only* in women, but certain personality traits exist in men and women to different degrees. Across societies, there are few differences in sex-typed behavior between boys and girls in the first six years. But by age seven, boys are more dominant and attention seeking and girls more nurturant. Across cultures, one pattern is virtually universal. Boys are more aggressive than girls. Aggression is the one behavior that consistently differentiates boys and girls at all ages.

The precise amount and type of sex-role difference varies with the type of society. The typical pattern in primitive societies is for men's work to be strenuous, cooperative, and require long periods of travel. Women's work is mainly associated with food gathering and preparation, crafts, clothing manufacture, and child care. It is not hard to see how this general pattern of differences holds true in more industrialized societies, although in these modern times it is changing.

Across cultures, boys learn to be overwhelmingly more achievement-oriented and self-reliant than girls. Similarly, girls learn to be overwhelmingly more nurturing than boys. Societies vary in the amount of aggression or passivity they consider normal, but within each particular society the men are more aggressive than the women. This balance between passive and aggressive behavior holds true universally.

## Nature or Nurture?

Boys and girls are different in several ways right from birth. Male infants are more active, cry more, and are more inquisitive than female infants. They are less easily frightened and more able to stand separation from their mothers. But adults also treat male and female infants differently right from birth. They allow boys to cry longer than girls before they offer comfort. Adults play more roughly with boys than girls. Adults encourage boys to play more actively and explore more than girls. On the other hand, they cuddle girls more than boys.

I have talked with many parents who are struggling to raise their children without gender stereotypes. These parents are frustrated because, despite their best efforts, their children favor gender-specific toys. Deprived of gender-specific toys, their children create them. Little girls cradle toy trucks as if they were dolls. Little boys use their dolls as if they were guns. Invariably the parents ask me whether the temperamental difference between boys and girls is genetic. My answer is yes and no. I always encourage these parents to continue doing their best to provide a nonsexist environment. But cultural stereotypes are all-pervasive; it is impossible for parents to insulate their children from them. They are unintentionally transmitted by caregivers, teachers, television, and even by parents themselves.

In a telling experiment,[3] researchers dressed two infants, one male, one female, in clothes that were identical except for their color. First, the researchers dressed the male infants in blue and the females in pink. Then they switched the clothes. They dressed the boys in pink and the girls in blue. Each time, the researchers asked adult subjects which baby was prettier and which was stronger. Adults, both men and women, consistently chose the baby dressed in blue as stronger and the baby in pink as prettier.

The conclusion of the child-development experts is clear: it is impossible to separate the influences of nature and nurture. Gender differences are a result of some combination and interaction between the two.

## At Our Core

Psychiatrists Jean Baker Miller, Janet L. Surrey, and others at the Stone Center for Developmental Services and Studies at Wellesley College are among the leaders in the field of gender differences in child development.[4] Their invaluable insights provide the foundation of our understanding how and why men and women are so different.

All humans need a sense of identity. Our sense of identity is what makes each of us unique. The way a child develops that sense of identity determines the way the adult will approach the world. Boys and girls develop their sense of self very differently. This creates a fundamental difference in the way men and women view the world and in the kinds of behaviors and relationships each finds comfortable. These differences affect the way men and women function in the workplace.

Why is there a fundamental difference in identity formation between boys and girls? The main reason is that it is women who are mothers and women who are usually the primary caretakers. Initially, the most important person to any child is his or her mother. The first person any child identifies with is Mother. Little girls can learn to become women by copying their mothers—but little boys can't learn to be men by copying their mothers even though they want to. Learning to become a man means learning to be very careful to be "different from Mother." A boy develops his identity by differentiating himself from everything female.

Because girls can identify with their mothers, girls base their identity on relationships and attachment. At the core of a woman's identity is a "self-in-relation."[5] Because women identify with the caregiver, girls learn caregiving. Girls learn the importance of putting others first. In a healthy home, they learn to be caring, giving, empathetic, and, to various extents, compliant.

For women, the world centers on people and relationships. They learn to be sensitive to the interrelationships between people and to value and maintain these relationships. Women are constantly aware of how their behavior affects other people. To a woman, the world is a web of relationships.

For boys, it is just the opposite. Because boys have to suppress their desire to identify with their mothers, they must reject feminine traits vigorously. They must devalue caring, giving, empathy, and compliance. Male identity formation depends on separation, on defining and stressing differences. At the core of a man's identity is a self that denies relatedness.

For men, the world centers on actions and the results of these actions. Relationships, in and of themselves, are not important. What is important is how these relationships affect outcomes.

Karen Horney, one of the first female psychoanalysts, described the differences in male and female development as the difference between "being" and "doing." Horney recognized that female identity is "ascribed" while male identity has to be "achieved."[6] Women are women because of what they are, men are men because of what they do. A woman's identity as a woman is based simply on the fact that she can bear children, just like her mother. A man's identity as a man is based on his continually proving his difference from his mother, from women.

This male-female difference in identity formation was brought home to me in a conversation with my crew on the way home from a race. The men were involved in an animated discussion of the latest video arcade game. When I asked what all the fuss was about, twelve-year-old Isaac, our fearless foredeck crew, explained the men's enthusiasm to me.

"It's human nature. You aren't a man until you shoot at something."

## CHAPTER TWO

# Games, Games, Games

## Boys' Games and Girls' Games

Child-development experts call play "the work of childhood."[1] Children form their identities through the games they play. While they are playing, children are developing and exercising the physical, mental, and social skills they will need as adults. The skills we learn in our childhood games form the foundation of our work style as adults.

Psychologists Carol Nagy Jacklin and Eleanor Maccoby study and write extensively about differences in male-female development and socialization.[2] They have found significant differences between the sexes. Almost from the beginning, children prefer playmates of their own sex. By the time they are four, children choose playmates of their own sex three times as often as opposite-sex playmates. By the time they are seven, this difference increases to eleven times.

These all-boy and all-girl groups develop very different styles of interaction. In their separate groups, boys and girls play games that encourage different competencies and different skills. Because boys' games are a closer approximation to the workplace than girls' games, boys learn skills that they will eventually use as adults in the workplace. The skills girls learn in their games are useful at home and in personal relationships, but not at work.

In their games, boys learn about conflict and competition. They learn the importance of resolving conflict and they learn conflict-resolution skills. They learn to fight and to play with their enemies. Because they play in large, heterogeneous groups and their games require coordinating the activities of many diverse people, boys learn leadership and organizational skills. They learn how to attain and maintain one's status in the male hierarchy. Boys' games take place primarily away from home—in streets, parks, and other public places—so boys learn to separate their home life from their play, and later their work, life.

Team sports are the most important games boys play, but all boys play some form of sports. A few of the men I interviewed told me they never played competitive sports. When I questioned them more closely, it became clear that while they did not play high-school varsity or college sports, as children these men played softball, were in Little League, played competitive games in gym class, or enjoyed less physically competitive games, like marbles. Even men who did not like playing competitive sports as children found playing competitive games inevitable. It is practically impossible for a boy to grow up in America without playing some competitive games. You have only to look at the media or listen to any group of boys or men talk to realize that competitive sports are part of the fabric of life.

Girls' games teach a completely different style of interaction. Girls' games stress the importance of cooperation and the development of noncompetitive skills. Games like house or dolls are role-playing games with no competitive aspects. In their competitive games, like hopscotch, girls learn individual rather than group skills.

Because they play in small cooperative groups, girls aren't forced to learn organizational skills. Girls have no reason to learn to play by the kind of complicated and rigid rules that a large group of boys need to play team sports. Playing house involves just a few people who are trying to be cooperative, so it requires very few rules. Their games take place close to home, so girls don't learn to separate home life and play life.

Girls downplay the importance of winning, because, for girls, maintaining relationships is more important than proving their superiority. They learn to compliment each other for the improvement in their skills, regardless of who wins. Girls experience very little conflict in their groups because girls' groups are so homogeneous and their games have few rules to break. But this means girls have very little opportunity to learn how to resolve conflict. Instead, girls learn to avoid rather than resolve conflict.

The difference between the way boys and girls resolve conflict is as striking as its consequences. In 1976, Dr. Janet Lever studied differences between boys' and girls' games.[3] She noticed that boys' games last longer than girls' games, not because they are more complicated, but because boys can resolve disputes. Boys quarrel much more than girls, but when boys quarrel, they find a way to resolve the quarrel and continue the game. They repeat the play by calling a "do-over," or debate which rules apply to the infraction. Girls' games are shorter because when girls quarrel, they end the game. They pick up their toys and go home.

Rules are more important to boys than to girls. Boys try to play by the rules of their games to the letter, but will argue with each other about exactly what these rules are. If they are unhappy with the result of a rule, boys will debate the applicability of that rule or try to find a loophole. Dr. Lever noted that boys seem to enjoy these debates as much as they enjoy playing the game itself. Girls, on the other hand, value relationships more than rules. They are willing to sacrifice rules to maintain relationships. If following a rule will endanger a relationship or hurt someone's feelings, girls will simply ignore the rules or make up new ones.

As adults, men carry their reliance on, and respect for, rules with them from their childhood games to the workplace. In the workplace men enjoy debating the precise meaning of the rules as much as they did as children. As adults, women still value relationships over arbitrary rules. They feel frustrated by rigid rules and would prefer to change or eliminate unhelpful rules rather than play by them. But because the workplace is still, for the most part, male-dominated, the rules are sacrosanct. You cannot break or change the rules to avoid hurting someone, but you can learn to bend them. An understanding of the rules, an appreciation of the importance men place on them, and the ability to manipulate the rules are essential skills for women in the workplace.

## Male and Female Definitions of Morality

Children develop and practice their understanding of morality in their play. The very different games boys and girls play encourage them to develop dramatically different definitions of morality. In 1982, Dr. Carol Gilligan published *In a Different Voice*, a groundbreaking study exploring and defining these differences between male and female moral development.

Psychologists test moral development by presenting children with moral dilemmas and rating their solutions on a carefully designed scale of moral development. A typical question—taken from a classic study by Dr. Lawrence Kohlberg—goes like this:

Mrs. Heinz is very sick and will die if she does not get a particular drug. This drug is very expensive. Mr. Heinz does not have enough money to buy the drug and the druggist refuses to lower the price of the drug. Should Mr. Heinz steal the drug?[4]

Dr. Gilligan found that boys resolved this dilemma easily, but girls were stymied. The boys approached this dilemma in a single-minded manner. For them, the question becomes the relative importance of property: stealing the drug, or saving Mrs. Heinz's life. Because life is more important than property, boys easily conclude that Heinz should steal the drug. They say it is proper for Heinz to steal the drug because otherwise his wife would die. The boys also say that if Heinz is caught stealing, he should be tried in court. They believe the judge will let Heinz off or give him a light sentence because Heinz did the right moral thing.

Rather than focusing on saving Mrs. Heinz's life, the girls focus on how stealing the drug would affect the relationships of the people involved. Instead of weighing the relative value of property verses life, they struggle to find a solution that would hurt neither the druggist nor Heinz's wife. Because theirs is an impossible goal, the girls could not find a satisfactory resolution to Heinz's dilemma.

The girls tried to resolve the dilemma by proposing that Heinz convince the druggist to give his wife the drug or go to the bank and get a loan. Because these were not options, the girls were stuck. They did not think that Heinz should steal the drug because they were unwilling to take anything from the druggist and were concerned that Heinz might go to jail.

Female morality evaluates the rules in the context of the situation. The girls stubbornly insisted that the rule should be that the druggist give Heinz the drug even though the dilemma precluded it. It is painful to watch the girls flounder over this life-and-death decision while the boys resolve it so easily. It reminds me of the many times I have heard women complain that a business decision is unfair, but offer no alternative because every viable solution requires hurting someone.

This dilemma illustrates the striking difference between the way boys and girls view rules. Boys value rules. They know that stealing is wrong and that people who are caught stealing will be arrested. When boys are unhappy with the results of the rules, they keep the rules but search for loopholes. They expect that the judge will find an excuse to let Heinz go free.

Girls see rules as a means to an end. They view the usefulness of rules by the context. Girls do not expect rules to be inviolate. They are comfortable discarding rules they find unhelpful or destructive. In the Heinz dilemma, they discard as irrelevant the rules that say you have to pay for drugs and banks will only give loans to people that can pay them back.

Dr. Gilligan's study illuminates the reason men and women find the others' idea of a moral solution so confusing. The moral imperative for men is that no one be deprived of his individual freedom. In the Heinz vignette, the druggist has a right to withhold the drug. For women, morality is fulfilling one's responsibility to the world, ensuring that no one gets hurt. The druggist should want to give Heinz the drug.

The morality of the workplace is male morality, based on the importance men place on laws and logic. The impact of solutions on human relationships does not enter the equation. For men, the primacy of the bottom line makes sense.

The Heinz dilemma illustrates what happens when these different moral views collide. The girls keep hoping that the druggist will see the light and help Heinz. What they don't understand is that the druggist sees his own kind of light and sees no reason to change his position. So understanding male morality is an essential tool for women. You have a much better chance of convincing a man to change his position if you can understand how he got there.

## Girls' Groups and Boys' Groups

Another consequence of the segregation of the sexes in childhood is that men and women develop very different styles of relating and communicating in groups. Dr. Deborah Tannen's books *You Just Don't Understand* and *Talking from 9 to 5* detail these differences at home and at work. When men and women come together in the workplace, they each bring their distinctive—and conflicting—communication styles. The result is frustration and confusion.

Psycholinguists study communication by recording and then analyzing conversations in boys' and girls' groups.[5] They find striking differences. In their groups, girls pay attention to relationships. They use conversation to develop and maintain social bonds, and work to maintain the group's cohesiveness and positive feeling. Girls always have a double agenda—to be "nice" and sustain social relationships as well as to achieve their own individual ends. Girls get their way by stressing agreement and group functioning and trying to avoid coercion and dominance.

In their groups, boys focus on dominance. Boys use conversation for egoistic purposes, for self-aggrandizement, and to establish and protect their turf. They have a single agenda: self-assertion. They get their way by using commands, boasts, and threats of authority.

Because girls and boys put such conflicting emphasis on relationships and dominance, they interact very differently. For example, before beginning to speak, a girl will acknowledge what the previous speaker has said and express agreement with another speaker before contradicting her. Boys simply make their point. Boys interrupt each other; girls pause to give each other a chance to speak. Girls soften their directives and involve their partners in the process of planning. Boys just give information or tell their partners what to do.

Girls politely listen to each other and make supportive and encouraging comments. Boys heckle speakers, tell jokes, and try to top each other's stories. They call each other names and refuse to comply with another's demands. When conflict occurs, girls try to smooth the waters; boys use threats and physical force to resolve it.

Boys do function effectively in groups despite their confrontational style, as evidenced by a sports team or an army unit. Boys' groups are not regulated by a concern for others' feelings as girls' groups are. Their groups function by maintaining a strict adherence to the rules. Men need rigid group structure, well-defined roles, dominance hierarchies, and team spirit to keep them interacting effectively. This is the hierarchical style of the workplace.

## Boys and Girls Together

Given their different interaction styles, what happens when boys and girls play together? The same thing that happens in the workplace: the boys take control. I am always astonished by how early children begin to conform to sex-role stereotypes. In their own groups, four-year-old girls are not passive. But in mixed groups, the girls stand on the sidelines and let the boys monopolize the play.

By age three, boys and girls are using very different methods to influence their play partners [6]—the same methods they will use as adults. Three-year-old girls make polite suggestions, while three-year-old boys make direct demands. Girls use phrases like "If you don't mind, would you please . . . ?" or even more indirectly, "Gee, I wish I had . . ." Boys say, "Get me that!"

The boys become increasingly less responsive to the girls' polite suggestions as they get older. By the time they are four, boys will not stop a behavior if asked by a girl, but *will* respond to the same demand when made by a boy. This pattern continues into adulthood, with disastrous results for women in the workplace. Have you ever been in a group that ignores a suggestion you made and then responds when a man makes the same suggestion?

Given this interaction pattern, it is hardly surprising that little girls find playing with boys aversive and avoid playing with them. But because they avoid these unpleasant interactions with boys, most girls never learn an effective way to cope with the boys' behaviors. The only women I interviewed who do not have problems interacting with groups of men either had all brothers or grew up in a neighborhood where there were no girls close by. These women were forced to play with boys as children and learned effective ways to deal with them.

Men and women bring the patterns of moral judgment, relating, and communicating they learned as children to the workplace. But the workplace is a male phenomenon. It functions in the same style boys learn in their childhood play, in the same style they use in their sports teams and in war. Men relate to each other just as they did as boys. This puts women who try to relate in their customary female style at a significant disadvantage. By understanding how and why men interact as they do, you can learn to work effectively with them.

## CHAPTER THREE

# Business Is a Game

Think of business as a game. Men do. Men approach their work with the same mind-set that they use in competitive sports. Competitive sports, war, and the workplace are governed by a set of unwritten rules familiar to most men but unknown to most women. In order to be competitive in the game of "work," you have to learn the rules of the game.

I asked the men I interviewed what they meant by "game." They defined a game as a contest of skills between opposing players. It is a discrete entity with a beginning and an end. Each game has its own set of rules. There are winners and losers in every game and the goal of a game is to win. This is as apt a definition for business as it is for football.

Games have a different meaning for men than for women, and are central to the way men relate. Girls learn to interact with each other by developing and maintaining relationships; boys learn to interact by playing games. In their games, boys learn to relate through domination and competition. They learn to see the world in an adversarial manner. Because they learn to relate around tasks and games, men are most comfortable interacting around concrete tasks and prefer structured, functional environments, like games or business.

Some men use work to avoid intimacy. These men prefer

staying at work to staying at home with their families. Work is a more comfortable setting for these men. They do not see the value of just talking, or just relating, and can't do it very well. They are most comfortable around people when they are performing a function in a structured environment like work or sports. Work and sports have rules to follow.

As children, boys idolize sports heroes. Sports provide a bond between fathers and sons. Men enjoy teaching their sons and applauding their competence in sports. In childhood, the community of boys and sports is what matters. In adulthood, it is the community of men and business.

You can hear the connection between the worlds of sports and business by listening carefully to the words men use when they speak to each other. How often have you heard businessmen use phrases like these to describe their business strategies?

"I'll have to go to the mat on this one."
"What's the battle plan?"
"He's playing hardball."

Pay attention to how often they pepper their anecdotes about work with sports and war analogies. Notice how they use the same approach and attitudes in war, games, and business.

A man's work is very important to him because men define themselves by their ability to meet their responsibilities and obligations. Work is the sector in which men achieve social status and is their main source of self-respect and feelings of worth. To men, being a good man means being able to maintain a respected place among men.

For men, games are serious business and business is a serious game. The men I interviewed are as successful in their sports as they are in their work. Successful men share an understanding of how to play the game, whether it be the sports game or the business game. This understanding makes them winners in all kinds of competitive situations. They are experts at the rules of the game.

## You Are Expected to Know the Rules

My neighbor Hal's exasperation trying to coach girls' soccer is a mirror of men's confusing experiences with women in business. Hal had been coaching the boys' soccer team. When he learned that the neighborhood wanted to create a girls' soccer team, he eagerly offered to coach it as well. Hal quit the girls' team after one season and swears he will never coach a girls' team again. The frustration he felt dealing with the girls is similar to the frustration men feel dealing with women in business.

He told me this story as an example:

> If a boy shows up late for practice, I make him do laps or extra sit-ups. The boys know this and do the laps or sit-ups with no complaints. I set the same rules for the girls, but when one of the girls showed up late, rather than do the required laps, she just cried. Her teammates told me I was unfair to make her cry. How did I make her cry? I don't understand. I thought they knew the rules.

Hal's understanding of the situation was that a player broke a rule and should accept the penalty. Hal expected her to forget about the situation as soon as she finished her penalty laps. I'm only guessing, but the girl probably thought that because he liked her, Hal would waive the penalty. She and her teammates interpreted Hal's sticking to the rules as a cruel sign that he did not like her anymore. The girls knew the rules of soccer, but they did not know the unwritten rules of the game.

You are expected to know two sets of rules when you play the game of business. One set of rules governs the skills of your trade. These are the skills they taught you in school, or later on the job. Women know these rules well. But there is another set of rules in effect that women don't know: the unwritten rules of the game. These rules are never mentioned explicitly, but men expect you to honor both sets of rules.

If you show up for a tennis match wearing whites and carrying an expensive tennis racket, your opponent will logically assume you know how to play. When you show up for work wearing a business suit and carrying a briefcase, your male coworkers will make the same assumption. They expect you to know and respect the rules of the game. Unfortunately, many women don't.

Even the most sympathetic men with whom I talked were puzzled by the way women behave in business. Countless times, men asked me to answer Freud's famous question: "What do women want?" I told them the answer is simple. Women are striving for the same goals men are. What confuses these men is the way women try to accomplish these goals.

I know from my experience in yacht racing how shocked men are when they finally realize you don't know the rules. When I began my informal study of the unwritten rules in racing, I asked my male crewmates a lot of questions. They were always willing to answer but often were incredulous. They thought I was kidding. I don't know how many times I heard "You didn't know that? Come on. Everyone knows that." Everyone doesn't, but everyone is expected to.

As adults, men carry their reliance on, and respect for, the rules with them from their childhood games to the workplace. In the workplace men enjoy debating the precise meaning of the rules as much as they did as children. As adults, women still value relationships over arbitrary rules.

Most women feel frustrated by rigid rules and would prefer to change or eliminate unhelpful rules rather than play by them. But the workplace is male-dominated and the rules are sacrosanct. You cannot break or change the rules to avoid hurting someone, but you can learn to debate a rule's applicability and look for loopholes. Understanding the rules, appreciating the importance men place on them, and being able to manipulate the rules are essential skills for the workplace.

## Stretching the Rules Is Part of the Game

Just how important rules are to men was brought home to me in a quote I noticed in the Sunday *New York Times Magazine*. It was part of a cooking article lavishly illustrated with pictures of sumptuous foods.

The author, William Grimes, an editor of the magazine, writes about cooking with his wife:

> . . . Which brings me to conflict area No. 2: the role of the recipe. I am appalled by her cavalier approach. She measures by hand, substitutes ingredients on a whim, overrules printed cooking times. *She does not go by the book,* which to me is the same as not playing by the rules.[1]

For men, rules are as important in the kitchen as they are on the football field or in editing a magazine.

Not only is it essential to know the rules, it is also imperative to understand the way men use rules. While women try to consider every situation in its own context, men consider every situation according to the rules. While women are checking to see if anyone is getting hurt, men are checking to see if everything is fair according to the rules.

But men do not blindly follow every rule. They have ways to manipulate the rules they don't want to follow. I think of this as stretching, but not breaking, the rules. When women don't like rules, they try to change them—just as Mrs. Grimes changed the recipe. But to men, this is breaking the rules. Men get around rules they don't want to follow by looking for a loophole. If, rather than just substituting ingredients, Mrs. Grimes created a loophole such as "This rule doesn't apply on humid days," then Mr. Grimes would have been more comfortable.

Part of the game is getting as close to breaking the rules as possible without actually breaking them. This is a difficult concept for most women to understand, yet mention it to a man and he will know exactly what "stretching the rules" means. The reason for this confusion is that women are trying to follow the spirit of the law while men are obeying the law to the letter.

My friend Robert inadvertently helped me illustrate this. Over dinner he confessed his desire to lose weight and asked for my help. I saw him eyeing the dessert cart. "Nothing from that cart," I said, before excusing myself to say hello to a friend at another table. I returned to find him eating ice cream. He grinned sheepishly and said, "It wasn't on the cart."

The practice of law is a profession built on the concept of stretching, but not breaking, the rules. The law is a set of rules. These rules are inviolate. But if you can convince the court that there is a different way to interpret the meaning of the words of the rule, you can achieve a different result. Lawyers arguing constitutional law debate precisely what the founding fathers meant by the way they worded the Constitution. A clever lawyer will try to change the meaning of a rule by reinterpreting a few sentences.

Admittedly, some of the conflict between men and women in business is a result of men's resentment of women in the workplace, but not all of it is. Some of this conflict and hostility is caused by the misunderstandings that result from men's and women's different assumptions about the function of rules. Because of the importance they place on rules, men resent women for not honoring and not playing by these rules. Because they are unaware of the way men value and manipulate the rules, women misinterpret men's behavior as personally hostile when it is simply the way men use the rules.

At present, the workplace is controlled by men. The workplace functions in a male style, by a set of unspoken male rules. If you want to play the game on the same playing field as the men, you have to know the rules—and how to manipulate them.

## The Object Is to Win

The best way I can explain the different way men and women feel about winning is with a personal experience:

> Part of the fun and the skill of sailboat racing is being able to respond to the unexpected and to overcome adversity. Unexpected problems occur constantly. During a major race on the Chesapeake Bay, the halyard (the rope that holds up the sails) on my boat broke.
>
> My sail fell down and I had to limp back to port to fix it. By the time we got back to the racecourse, the other boats were out of sight. Needless to say, we did not win that race. My crew certainly wasn't happy, but we all knew that facing situations like this is part of the game.

Compare this with my experience in a sailboat racing course given by and for women. All-women events are fun and valuable for confidence building, but this experience is all too typical.

> During the last race of the series, a halyard broke on one of the boats and its sail fell down. Because the crew had to stop to fix the halyard, this boat finished last. The regatta organizers felt so sorry for them that they decided to change the rules.
>
> The organizers decreed that this team could replace their score on this race with the average of their scores in other races. This change allowed this crew to win the first-place trophy rather than the fourth-place trophy they would have won on the real racing circuit. The organizers were more concerned with comforting the women on the damaged boat than running an authentic regatta.

Whenever I tell this story to a man, he is horrified. "That's not fair" is his usual response. Men cannot understand why no one objected, especially the women on the second-place boat who really won the regatta. Why didn't they violently object to having first place taken away from them? Men cannot fathom why these women were willing to forgo winning to avoid hurt feelings. For men the object of the game is to win, not to make sure that everybody is content.

I was impressed by a comment made by Andre Agassi in an interview after losing a tennis match. "The best thing besides playing and winning is playing and losing," he said.

He didn't say just "playing." When you play, you end up either a winner or a loser. For him, winning and losing are part of the game.

The difference in male and female attitudes about winning is a result of our childhood games. Boys are playing games that are contests between partners, while girls are playing games that are cooperative and skill building. Girls' games are usually designed so that everybody gets a prize or everybody gets to win. But in boys' games there are winners and losers.

Even when men and women play the same games, they play them with different goals. In tennis, for example, two women often opt to volley the ball or not keep score, while two men usually prefer to play a game. Men consider volleying to be a way to practice and master a stroke, not an end in itself. The goal of playing tennis for men is to win.

In the work world, the equivalent of volleying may get your work done, but it won't get you promoted. If your goal is to be promoted, you have to confront your reluctance to compete. Are you afraid to lose—or are you afraid you will win? For most women, the answer is both. Competition puts women in a double bind.

Winning for women becomes a mixed pleasure because women are trained not to hurt anyone's feelings. It is impossible to enjoy winning if you are concerned that by winning, you have hurt your opponent's feelings. If you are concerned that the people you triumph over will not like you, you have no choice but to be a loser. In order to compete to win, you have to learn to tolerate other people's discomfort and dislike.

Another problem for women is that in our culture, competence is not feminine—particularly if it means demonstrating greater competence than a man. The cultural imperative is for women to make men feel strong, not to point out a man's weakness. And the aggression a woman needs to win is likely to be criticized.

If you want to win, you *have* to be willing to defeat your opponent. If there are winners, there have to be losers. Your winning does not have to humiliate the other person. If it does, either you are not a good winner or your opponent is not a good loser.

# Concentrate Only on the Game While You Are Playing It and Forget About the Game When You Go Home

Men separate the game of business from the rest of their lives the same way they separate one game from another. Work is just another game to be played.

This is easier to understand if you apply it to your company softball league. When it is time to play, you put on your team T-shirt and sneakers, pick up your bat and glove, and go out to the ball field. You concentrate on playing your position and trying your best. After nine innings, the team with the most runs wins. Then you go home.

Leaving your work behind you when you go is easier said than done. But separating your work from the rest of your life will help you play your best. It underscores the difference between who you are and your role in the game. This separation enables you to play by different rules at work than at home. It is easier to play by rules you don't like if you know you will leave them behind when you go. If you win, you get a trophy to take home to remind you of your success. If you lose, you can leave your failures behind you when you leave.

To help you separate the game from the rest of your life, associate some objects and places with work, and only work. Uniforms help. If you wear certain clothes only at work, you will find yourself focused on work when you wear them. The same is true for places. If you only work in certain places, you will be focused on work when you are in your work places. Rituals are also a big help. Sit down to a quiet cup of tea, enjoy a hot bath, work out at the gym, or just go for a walk around the block to signal the end of the workday. You will be surprised how much easier this makes leaving work behind.

Men joke about women's interest in clothes, but have you ever tried to throw out a man's favorite shabby sweater? Men know that putting on a favorite sweater will help them relax. Men who balk at dressing up during weekends are balking because suits are "work uniforms." Changing clothes the minute they get home helps them know which role they are in. When men work at home, they go to a specific room of the house, usually a study or home office, where they work and expect to be uninterrupted. Only when they emerge from their office are they really at home.

So try to create a distinct difference in your wardrobe between your work clothes and the clothes you relax in. Even your dress clothes should have a different flavor from the clothes you work in. And take off your work clothes as soon as you get home. If you must work at home, create the same distance that men create. Make a part of your home your work space, and don't let anyone interrupt you.

As for concentrating only on your work when you are working, it is a difficult habit to master. Women's roles overlap more than men's roles. The job of mother, for example, is twenty-four hours a day.

You can forget about your home while at work only if someone else is taking care of household and child-care responsibilities. Unfortunately, even when they have partners, most women still have the primary responsibility for their homes and children. I have heard men talk about "baby-sitting" their children, as if the prime responsibility for their child lay elsewhere. Too many men proudly brag about "helping with the housework," not realizing they are saying that the real responsibility for the house remains with their partner even though she works as long a day as he does.

Business is unsympathetic to women who have other responsibilities to balance. Simply caring for other responsibilities can be interpreted as a betrayal. That is how the game has been played up until now. This attitude is beginning to change, but change is slow. Unfair as it may seem, caring about a home life is not part of the game.

Since your responsibilities are not going to disappear, you have to find a way to appear as if you only concentrate on work when you are working. Remember, it only has to *seem* as if you are giving work all your attention. If other responsibilities must intrude into your work time, camouflage them. You will be astonished at how much respect you will earn from men if they think you are putting your work first.

## When the Game Is Over, Be Friends with Your Opponent

Helen, a corporate attorney, describes her first negotiation:

> The two sides disagreed so violently that I imagined I heard growling and saw bared teeth. At one point I tried to intervene when my partner, Doug, and the attorney representing the other side got into a shouting match. They just ignored me.
>
> When we finally reached an agreement, I expected to go out and celebrate with Doug. But instead, I watched him walk out, laughing and joking with the man he had been yelling at just a few minutes before.

This scene is familiar in sports. How many times have you seen groups of boys competing against each other in sports and then all going out together after the game?

When I began racing, I was appalled by the way sailors shouted at each other; I now know where the expression "swearing like a sailor" comes from. But when the races are over, the same sailors always get together for a party. One skipper explained it this way: "None of the anger crosses the finish line."

Helen wondered how Doug and his opponent could forgive each other after their violent disagreement. But she's missing the point. The men don't forgive each other, because there is nothing *to* forgive! In the context of their negotiation, their argument was simply appropriate behavior. Their hostile behavior was just part of the game. Once the negotiation was over, they were no longer opponents.

As children, boys learn to be friends with their opponents. Their games are more competitive, violent, and conflictual than girls'. If little boys did not become friends with their opponents, they would soon have no friends, because their opponents one day are their teammates the next. Out of necessity, the boys learn to separate their play from their friendships. Because little girls avoid conflict in their games, they have no compelling reason to learn this separation.

The better you are at separating yourself from your role at work, the more natural it becomes to be friends with your opponent. In a competitive situation, your goal is to win. If acting offensively helps you win, then offensive behavior may be an appropriate part of the game. But remember, direct the abuse at your competitor in the game, not at your opponent as a person. And when the game is over, be friends.

## SUMMARY

Think of business as a game.

1. You are expected to know the rules.

2. Stretching the rules is part of the game.

3. The object is to win.

4. Concentrate only on the game while you are playing it and forget about the game when you go home.

5. When the game is over, be friends with your opponent.

# PART TWO

# LEARNING THE RULES OF THE GAME OF "WORK"

# Introduction

Unwritten rules form the foundation for the practice of business. Men have been practicing these unwritten rules of the game all their lives, but these rules are new to most women. Nobody directly teaches these rules to boys. Boys absorb them by example while playing sports, and then comfortably transfer these rules from their games to their work. The rules feel so natural that it would never occur to a man to explain them to you; he assumes you, too, already know them.

I did not make up the rules that I am going to share with you. These rules are a synthesis of the material I gathered in my interviews with successful men. Some of them were familiar to me as the rules of good sportsmanship, but others were a surprise. You may not like these rules, but it is essential you understand them.

My purpose in offering you these rules is not to encourage you to act like men. It is to help you understand men and the rules they work by. When you know the rules, you can anticipate men's behavior, giving you an edge in negotiations and competition. The business world will make more sense to you. You will feel a reduction in your level of stress. You can avoid hostility created by inadvertently breaking rules you never knew existed. You instantly will get along better with your male coworkers. Understanding the rules gives you the opportunity to evaluate male and female ways of viewing the world and to pick the best of each.

In this section I will explain the rules to you the way the men explained them to me. You will like some of these rules, for they represent a healthy approach to life, but others you may find reprehensible. How can you follow rules you hate? You can't *change* the rules you don't like, but you can find a way *around* them.

Always keep in mind that you can't break the rules, but you can stretch them. Do what men do when faced with rules they don't want to follow: Find a loophole. Be creative with the rules. Adapt the rules in a way that fits you. Brainstorm with other women. I'll share the loopholes and effective ways of stretching the rules that I have learned. With some creativity, you can find an acceptable and effective way to play by the rules and win.

These rules do need changing. There are serious flaws in the way the world does business. The workplace can and should be humane as well as efficient. But the most effective way to promote change is from a position of power. Understanding the rules will help you achieve success in the business world. When you become powerful, I hope you will use your power to bring about the positive long-term changes the world of business needs. As more women break the glass ceiling, we can work together to rewrite the rules.

But until then, here are the rules of the game.

## CHAPTER FOUR

# Rule 1:
# Act Competent

Susan is a staff member in the marketing department of a large corporation. She has been producing excellent work in this position for the past six years. When a new position one level above hers became available, Susan applied for it, confidently expecting to be chosen for the job. She knew she was the most experienced and the most competent candidate. The position went to Harry, a less experienced, less competent coworker who has been with the company for less than a year.

Why did this happen?

Harry was not as skilled or as talented as Susan. He did not work as long or as hard as Susan. Susan often stayed late to produce a quality product. Harry stayed late less often than Susan—but when he did, he made sure his managers knew about it. Like everyone else, Harry made mistakes—but he never mentioned those mistakes to anyone. Harry *did* make sure everyone knew when he successfully completed a project. He never refused to accept a project regardless of whether or not he had any idea how to do it. He rarely asked for help. Harry looked as if he worked hard, made few mistakes, was successful at all his projects, and was expert at everything he did.

Susan did not know about Rule 1: Act competent.

Harry knew that "acting competent" is part of the game. The operative word in this rule is the word "act." Acting and posturing are some of the skills of this game. Bluffing is a part of this game. If you can convince your manager that you are competent when you are not, well, that is also part of the game.

Since Harry knew that the way to get promoted was to convince his superiors that he was the best person for the job, that is what he did.

Playing competitive sports in large groups is the training ground for acting competent. In boys' games, only the best players play; the rest sit on the bench. For boys, just being chosen becomes an end in itself. Girls generally do not face the same amount of pressure to be chosen in their games. To avoid hurting anyone's feelings, girls make an effort to give everyone a chance to play. But if your goal is to be chosen for a team, being perceived as competent is every bit as important, or more important, than being competent. Boys who want to be picked for a team thus learn the importance of playing a new game called "how competent can you make everyone think you are?" Because girls know they will get a chance to play regardless, they never need to learn this new game.

Just as women are handicapped by cultural pressure to look weak, men are handicapped by cultural pressure to look strong and in command. Part of the definition of being a man is always knowing what to do, always taking the lead. When boys are struggling to develop their identities as men, they often fake something rather than admit they do not know it. They equate "not knowing" with being a girl. Boys thus learn the effectiveness of "acting" competent very early in life. It becomes a valued skill.

Our society traditionally defines females as the weaker sex.

Just as boys learn to act strong if they are not strong, girls learn to act weak if they are not weak. In order to look feminine, girls are encouraged to hide their competence. By adulthood, women have become accustomed to pretending to look uncertain about their competence. Unfortunately, in many settings it does make the men around them feel more comfortable. It may comfort your supervisor to think he is smarter than you, but it will not persuade him to promote you.

In an enlightening study of hiring practices, subjects were given descriptions of applicants' work performance and asked to rate these applicants. All the raters were given the same descriptions, but the researchers told half of the raters that the applicant was a man and told the other half of the raters that the applicant was a woman. Even though the descriptions were exactly the same, the raters judged the men as more competent.[1] To be judged as equally competent as men, women have to do a job that is more exceptional.

Women have complained to me that even when they are radiating competence, some men still perceive them as less competent. Sometimes this is because of the cultural bias I just described, but other times it is because the women are not using the "appropriate" conventions men use to tell each other that they are competent. In many cases, what looks like bluster, rudeness, or even dishonesty to a woman looks like appropriate behavior to a man. To communicate your competence to a man, you have to act in a way that he will interpret as signaling competence.

I do not think Harry, whom we discussed earlier, is someone to be emulated. Being competent is much better than acting competent. But acting competent is an essential part of the game. I am not going to encourage you to fake your way through your career, but you can learn something from Harry.

There are times when it *is* essential to pretend to be more competent than you feel. If you are hesitant to "act" competent, ask yourself what the cost will be if you are wrong. If a mistake will ruin your career or if it is life threatening, don't risk it. But in most cases, the cost of an error is not that high. At these times I encourage you to "act." If you know you are competent, I also encourage you to make your competence visible. Don't assume that people are aware of your good work and your competence. You may have to convince them. Let me show you how.

## Act Like You Know What You're Doing, Even If You're Not Sure That You Do Know

Saul, an accomplished trial lawyer, describes how he felt when he started practicing law:

> I didn't know what I was doing. I felt frightened but I knew enough not to let my insecurities show. I felt it— but I just didn't show it. Then I discovered that no one else knew what they were doing either and I felt much better.

As soon as Saul learned that business played by the same unwritten rules as sports, he felt more comfortable. He knew he only had to *look* like he knew everything. Saul knew about acting competent, he just did not know that was what he was supposed to do at work.

Contrast this with how Martha felt when she began practicing law.

I wondered how classmates with so little training and experience knew enough to take on such hard tasks. They had the same background and training as I did, yet they seemed to know so much more. I wondered where I was when these skills were taught. I felt frightened for a long time.

Because sports traditionally are so much of a boy's upbringing, by adulthood men are experienced in the art of getting selected for a team. No one likes to be the last to be chosen. Most men have learned that one way to ensure that they are chosen is to know a lot about that sport. Another way to ensure selection is to look like you know a lot about that sport. Saul realized that the same principle was operative in his work, but Martha believed everyone actually knew as much as they pretended to know.

I have often encountered this phenomenon while racing my sailboat. Whenever I ask a new male crewmember to do something, I know he will say yes and try to do it. As a new crewmember, he will feel he has to prove himself by convincing me he is an expert at everything. Rather than ask how or what to do, he will just try *something*. This can be dangerous on a sailboat because if he guesses wrong he may endanger himself or the crew. Frightening as it seems, some men will risk making a dangerous mistake rather than admit that they do not know something.

Women do just the opposite. When I ask a new female crewmember to do something, she will ask how to do it. She will even ask if she has done it many times on another boat, just to be sure she does it exactly right. This is as dangerous as the male style because some tasks have to be done immediately. If she does not do it, a less experienced man might have to.

As a skipper, I have learned to counterbalance these response styles by dividing the knowledge new male crewmembers claim to have in half and doubling the knowledge new female crewmembers claim. I will encourage a new female crew to try something she has not done before because I know she will ask for help at the first sign of a problem. With a new male crewmember, I will provide extra backup until I am sure he knows what he is doing. This helps me get the best from my crew and still ensure the boat's safety. In business, managers are not going to make this adjustment for their staffs.

Alfred, an insurance executive, described his reaction to Annette's responses during her job interview. When Alfred explained that one of the responsibilities of the job would be contract negotiation, she said: "Oh, I've never done that before. I don't know if I can do it."

He was stunned. Annette thought she was being honest, but Alfred thought she was telling him that she was incompetent. He couldn't understand why she would think he would want to hire someone who couldn't do the job.

Before you say you cannot do something, ask yourself exactly what you mean when you say you don't know how to do it. Do you mean that you haven't a clue and have never seen it done? Do you mean you haven't been formally trained? Is it something you have never done but know how to look up or find out how to do?

Trust that you know enough about a subject to figure out what you don't know. Give it a try. Research it yourself. There is a first time for everything. You have done many things for the first time. Think about your accomplishments. You will be surprised how often you can accomplish your task without help. If you do need help, get it quietly.

If you respond to new assignments by saying "No problem!" rather than "How do you do that?" you will develop a reputation for having a can-do attitude. You will get a better year-end review if your supervisor relaxes when he gives you an assignment because he knows you will do it well than if you do an equally good job but he thinks you look uncertain.

## Ask for Help Only When You Really Need It

Phil and Lois were driving to an unfamiliar marina in a rural part of Maryland. Neither of them had been to that marina before and they knew they were lost. As is common in that part of Maryland, the roads they were driving on were too small to be on the map. Lois suggested they stop for directions. Phil was also frustrated, but unwilling to follow this suggestion. He grumbled at the car, at the directions, at Lois's map-reading ability. He blamed their situation on everything but his own refusal to stop.

Although it was not his fault they were lost, Phil felt responsible and incompetent. Lois knew that he would eventually ask for directions, and he did. But his sense of when it was time to ask was quite different from Lois's. Men don't ask questions until they have exhausted every other possibility. They *have* to try to solve the problem first, even if solving it is an impossibility. For men, asking for directions is an admission of defeat.

Men ask questions in a stylized way in an attempt to camouflage their feeling of ineptness. Lois would have said, "I'm lost; can you tell me how to find Harvey's Marina?" or "I've never been here before; can you tell me how to get to Harvey's Marina?" But to Phil, asking this way would have suggested weakness.

When Phil finally stopped for directions, he said, "I am looking for Harvey's Marina. I tried going west on Ashe and south on

Tilson, but I haven't found it yet." He phrased the question this way to communicate that the questioner was a man of action. It suggests that Phil was not facing the situation passively. He did not ask for help until he had exhausted his own repertoire of solutions. Phil would have also been comfortable asking in a way that clearly indicated that being lost was not his fault. These differences may seem subtle or unnecessary to you, but they affect the way men perceive each other, and the way they perceive you.

For men, asking questions is not just a means of getting information. It is also a way to signal dominance. Asking for information defines one as a subordinate. The person with the answer is the dominant one. And being dominant is primary for men. Dominance and competition underlie the way men relate. The man with the most knowledge has the most power. To look powerful, you must look knowledgeable. A woman is in her culturally defined role when she asks for information. Her role is to be passive, dependent, or weaker. For men, asking is in direct opposition to the cultural directive to be the biggest and the strongest.

Too often, women ask questions as if apologizing for asking. "Can I bother you a minute?" "Would you mind helping me?" These questions suggest there is something wrong with not knowing the information. If you do have to ask for help, and there are times when you'll need to, you want your question to imply that it is appropriate for you to ask. Ask in a confident manner, as directly as possible. "You have some information I need" or "I need this information" are appropriate. Stress the actions you have already taken to solve the problem. Practice asking with as few qualifiers and apologies as possible.

There are times when women use questions for reasons other than getting information. For women, asking questions can be a way of relating. A woman may ask a question as a way to start a conversation, to express concern, or to show interest. When you ask questions of a woman friend, she knows you are interested in her thoughts and she views you favorably. A man is likely to think you are nosy or insecure.

The statement "It never hurts to ask" is untrue. It depends on how you ask, why you ask, and when you ask. It doesn't hurt to ask if you are asking *for* something. It does hurt to ask if you show that you don't know something. So if you need information and there is no other way to get it, ask. But ask sparingly and confidently.

## Brag About Your Accomplishments and Flaunt Your Talents

Phyllis, an accountant in a large consulting firm, was collaborating with a colleague, Jerry, on an important presentation. She found Jerry to be lazy and not very bright. She had to do most of the work. As they had planned, Phyllis began the presentation, being careful to credit Jerry for any work he did do. During his portion of the presentation, Jerry never said a word about Phyllis's contributions. He did point out his own labor. Whenever possible, he allowed the audience to attribute work to him that had been done by Phyllis.

Guess who was congratulated for his good work and guess who was told she was a good helper?

Phyllis made it easy for Jerry to outshine her. She had done nothing either before the meeting or during it to suggest that the excellent presentation was primarily her work. How was anybody to know? Men *expect* you to make yourself visible. If you do not say you are the author of something, they assume you are not.

Women are used to sensing what is *under* the surface, but

men do not think that way. They only see what is *on* the surface. They accept what is shown them.

Audrey, a young lawyer who had several years of experience, was working with a male associate just out of law school. She knew she was a good lawyer. She was proud of her skills and assumed her colleagues would recognize them as well. Arthur, who was not very talented, bragged a lot about how good he was. Audrey found him annoying and abrasive. She was surprised to discover that the partners in her firm believed Arthur and liked his bragging. They responded to him as if he were as good as he claimed.

Men are much more comfortable bragging than women. As boys, they learn they have to brag. Boys who are trying to get picked for a team know that they will not get picked if no one knows them or if no one knows how well they play. So they learn to flaunt, and at times embellish, their accomplishments.

Children are taught that modesty is a virtue. But this rule seems to be taken to heart more by women than men. Our picture of male virility includes brashness and bravado, but our traditional picture of femininity includes unobtrusiveness, modesty, and timidity. One of the few times a man may act modest is when he does not flaunt an achievement that is so big that everyone knows about it anyway.

Women have been taught to hide their competence since childhood. Lyn Mikel Brown and Carol Gilligan followed the development of one hundred girls, ages seven to eighteen, as they entered and negotiated adolescence.[2] They watched as outspoken competent eight- and nine-year-olds became insecure, quiet young women, no longer comfortable speaking their minds. Girls learn boys won't like them if they are too smart, or too competent. For girls who insist on being good students, the message is to keep their achievements to themselves.

Hiding or downplaying your achievements is just the opposite of the bragging and flaunting that men and boys do. To look competent, you should brag about your accomplishments and flaunt your talents. You must let people know that you are competent. Be proud of your strengths. Let people know what you have accomplished.

## Don't Advertise Your Mistakes

Paul, a marketing executive, noticed a letter lying on my desk. It may have been impolite of him to read it, but he read it anyway. He asked me why I started it off with "I'm sorry it took me so long to get back to you."

I thought the answer was obvious. "Because it took me so long to get back to him."

I thought an apology was in order. Paul shook his head in disbelief. He patiently explained that if you don't call attention to how long overdue your reply is, your correspondent may not notice its lateness. If you mention it, he can't help but notice. If your correspondent does notice that your letter is late, he will soon forget it—unless he is reminded of your tardiness every time he pulls your file and sees this letter.

How impolite . . . and what a good idea. My letter is a good example of what men call "advertising your mistakes." It is easier for people to overlook or forget your mistakes if you let your mistakes fade from view rather than point them out.

Everyone makes mistakes. But everyone does not have to know about yours. I am not suggesting you hide or lie about your mistakes. I am simply suggesting that you refrain from bringing them up.

When I asked the men I interviewed if they told people about their mistakes, they were incredulous. Their almost universal answer was "of course not." They told me the only time it seemed appropriate to talk about their mistakes was when they were talking to someone who could help them correct them. Making mistakes makes you look incompetent. Talking about mistakes calls attention to your failings. Part of the formula for looking competent is to help people forget your mistakes.

Remember, the image you are trying to create is that of *competence*. You want people to notice your strengths and overlook your weaknesses. So hide, rather than highlight, those weaknesses.

## SUMMARY

RULE 1: ACT COMPETENT.

1. Act like you know what you're doing, even if you're not sure that you do know.

2. Ask for help only when you really need it.

3. Brag about your accomplishments and flaunt your talents.

4. Don't advertise your mistakes.

## CHAPTER FIVE

# Rule 2:
# Act Strong

*Keep a stiff upper lip.*
*Big boys don't cry.*
*Are you a man or a mouse?*

In our culture, strength is an essential component of masculinity. From childhood on, boys learn the importance of being strong. We urge little boys to eat their vegetables so they can grow up "big and strong." Clint Eastwood, Sylvester Stallone, and Arnold Schwarzenegger are among our male role models.

Of course, not all men are strong, and certainly men don't always feel strong. But men learn how to look and act strong. As in Rule 1: Act competent, the operative word in Rule 2: Act strong is "act."

## Always Try to Take Control and Be in Control

Janine, a TV producer, complained about her manager:

> I don't know what to do with him. He wants to know everything that goes on. He wants me to do everything

his way. I want to be in control of my own programs. When I ask him to put me in control, he always says okay, but then he interferes anyway. I keep asking for control—what else can I do?

Janine made a common but fatal error. She asked for control. The most important thing to remember about control is that nobody ever *gives* control to you. If someone gives you control, they are still in control. You have to *take* control.

Use this knowledge to your advantage. Believe it or not, an effective way to take control is to give it to the person who already has it. If you know that you are overpowered and your opponent is about to take control, ask him to take charge. If he takes control, he will be following your directions—ultimately leaving you in control.

For example, when Janine's manager was about to interfere, Janine could have taken control by saying in a strong confident voice, "I can tell you don't like the backdrop. Tell me how you want it changed." If he tells her, he is doing what she said. Although this sounds simple, it has a strong psychological effect. The words sound deferential, but the underlying message, the "meta-message," is that Janine is telling him what to do. In an attempt to get back in control, people often respond by saying "you do it." Either way you win.

The strongest person in any game is the person in control. When you control the game board, you can control the game. The person in control tailors the game to his advantage.

Control of information is a key element of power. You can only present your ideas to your boss if you can get an appointment with him. If you are not in control, your ideas, no matter how brilliant, may never be heard. Your arguments will be most persuasive if you can present them in the medium in which you are strongest. If you are more effective on paper than verbally, you want to control the situation to require arguments on paper. Be conscious of the fact that your opponent will be trying constantly to adapt the situation to his own advantage, so you have to turn the situation around to the way that will work best for you.

Many women feel uncomfortable taking charge of a situation without being given the official go-ahead. Since childhood, women have been encouraged to be followers. For many women, responding feels more natural than initiating. When you take control without permission, you run the risk of angering the powers that be. But the potential reward is worth the risk.

When you take control, you take responsibility. If something goes wrong, you will get the blame. But you also get the credit when you achieve your objective. If you feel it is impolite to tell someone else what to do, ignore your discomfort. Remind yourself that you are just doing your job. This kind of discomfort will diminish over time.

Anyone who takes control will encounter some resistance. When a woman takes control, she faces this natural resistance, but she also runs into an additional resistance. In our culture, the only woman allowed to tell a man what to do is his mother. Often unconsciously, men feel emasculated when commanded by a woman and will resist.

Matthew, a biotechnologist, confided:

> Anything but a polite request by a woman makes me bristle. I try to put that feeling aside and do what has to be done. But, yes, I have to put my emotions aside consciously.

A rule of thumb is that the more confident the man, the more he will welcome your taking control. Be alert if you are taking control from an insecure man. He is likely to resent you. There is nothing you can do about this except watch for the form his resentment takes and try to circumvent it.

If you are reluctant to take control, ask yourself if you expect people to be fair. You probably do. This assumption is more common among women than men. Unfortunately, this basic supposition is often wrong. In the business world, people are not always fair, or honest. You will be frustrated and angry if you expect them to be. Remind yourself that your taking control can then be a way to ensure fairness.

## Do Not Be Obviously Dependent on a Superior

Georgio, the owner of an international shipping company, told me how he evaluates women with whom he is considering doing business:

> I want someone who can stand up to her boss. That's one of the fears I have with working with a woman. I always worry that maybe the boss above isn't giving her enough respect. So I try to get them both together. And if I see her sit there and not say one word, then I don't think she's strong enough for me.

Georgio is concerned that a woman will not fight for his interests, especially with her superiors. He admitted that he does not put men through this test. Unfortunately, his prejudice is common. Men expect women to function well as a second in command, but not as leaders. To counter this image, you have to establish your independence very clearly.

Evaluate your behavior and be sure that you do not *look* dependent on a superior. Don't just be independent; make sure your independence is apparent. Express *your* opinions. Talk about decisions *you* will make, actions *you* will take. Men are hypersensitive to anything that looks like dependency in a woman.

To men, dependency is a sign of weakness. It is a clear signal that you do not have the strength to deal with a difficult situation on your own, that you will not fight when fighting is called for. Make it clear that you are making the decisions and that you will stand by your word.

There will be times when you will have to clear something with your supervisor. When this is the case, simply don't let your opponent know you need approval. Or at least be sure you do not call attention to it. Saying something innocuous like "I'll have to get back to you on that" is better than saying "I'll have to talk to a senior partner and see if he will okay it." Your clients want to know they can rely on *you* to get the job done.

## Do Not Let Your Opponent Know He Has "Gotten to You," Even If He Has

Brett, manager of an architecture firm:

I hate to see a woman cry, except when I want her to.

His statement is a chilling reminder of this part of the rule. Don't let your opponent know he's gotten to you when he has, and don't let him see you cry.

If a competitor senses that a tactic has worked on you, he will continue to use that tactic. In an argument, men feel it is a victory to fluster an opponent. If your opponent knows he's gotten to you, he will continue to do what you have shown him bothers you. Looking stoic is a difficult skill to cultivate, but a very valuable one.

One of the greatest tests of a man's strength is his ability to look cool in the face of adversity. If you can remember that business is a game, that it is only a game, that there is always another game tomorrow, it will be easier to keep your hurt from showing. In fact, the more you remember it is a game, the less hurt you will have to hide.

## Do Not Sulk or Complain If Things Do Not Go Your Way

While I was looking forward to my first experience skippering a week-long sailing trip, I received an unpleasant surprise. The boat I was to have chartered had been in an accident the week before. The only boat the charter agent had available was in sorry shape. It barely looked like it would stay afloat. I expected sympathy from the other skippers, all male, when I began to complain. Instead, they seemed annoyed and avoided me.

When I finally began to clean up the boat, Rock, one of the other skippers, came over to help. "Always remember," he said, "when life gives you lemons, make lemonade."

I immediately renamed my boat *Lemonade* and went on to enjoy a wonderful week. No one on that trip can remember the original name of that boat, but we all remember *Lemonade*.

In the situation above, I felt helpless and did not know how to change it. And no one helped me until I took action myself. I learned an important lesson through this: sulking and complaining are behaviors that go against the stiff-upper-lip ethic. Men are not supposed to show emotion. In business, as in sailing, neither are women.

Sulking and complaining are signs of powerlessness. When you are in control, sulking and complaining are unnecessary. Sulking and complaining are indirect ways of asking someone to change a situation you are too frightened to change or are convinced you can't change yourself. People complain and sulk when they feel powerless.

Men get angry when they see a woman sulking or complaining because they see these actions as indirect requests for help. Because men are raised to help women, they feel obligated to help, and in business, they resent it. When they see a man sulk or complain, men do not feel obligated to help him. They just label him "moody" or consider him weak. They are more likely to feel obligated to help him if he doesn't complain.

When you sulk or complain, you put the men around you in a double bind. They will resent you because they have enough of their own problems to fix. If they solve your problem, they have given you time that you don't deserve. But if they don't try to help you, they feel guilty. Either way, they resent you and you lose.

When you find yourself sulking or complaining, consider it a signal. It means you are in a situation that needs changing.

If you find yourself sulking, ask yourself if you are hoping that somebody will see you sulk and feel sorry for you. Remind yourself that the response you are most likely to encounter is resentment, not gallantry. Besides, why bother sulking? It is so much more productive to problem-solve and plan a solution. View the problem as a new challenge.

Yet we are all human, and all humans feel like sulking sometimes. Here are some tips on how to get yourself out of a sulk.

1. Go someplace where you can be alone. You can close your office door or seclude yourself in a stall in

the ladies' room. Try to feel as terrible as you can. Give yourself a specific amount of time—ten minutes is a good amount—to feel as bad as you like. Brood, think hopeless, angry thoughts, and try to keep yourself from thinking anything useful during that period of time. You will discover that you are relieved when your "brooding time" is over—and you can then act productively to solve the situation.

2. Take a brisk walk—around the office, if necessary. When you sulk, you usually sit still and stare at your hands or into space. It is extremely difficult to move around physically and sulk simultaneously. A brisk walk will raise your energy level and help you clear your head to problem-solve.

3. Shift your attention to someone or something else. If you can, talk to somebody about something else— about the weather, if necessary. Make a quick phone call to a friend. If there is no one available, stop thinking and look around. Distract yourself by thinking about what is going on in the room around you.

Sulking is a silent request for help, but complaining is a not-so-silent request. When you complain, you are indirectly asking someone to change something for you. If you are complaining and not changing the situation yourself, you are probably afraid of someone or something. Ask yourself, who or why? Is it really so fearful?

If you are complaining, there is something you are having difficulty accomplishing. Can the person to whom you are complaining be helpful? Do you want him to do something? If so, ask him directly, instead of taking the roundabout route. What is it that you want to change? Why do you want to change it? Why can't you change it yourself?

We feel we are unable to change a situation because we feel

powerless. If you feel you can't change something, remember: Little girls are powerless; women are not.

The worst that can happen to you if you ask for something is that someone will say no. Replace any thoughts that inhibit you from acting with this one:

> It is inexcusable not to try to remedy any situation you
> do not like.

Tell someone *directly* when they offend you and tell them *directly* how you want them to treat you. Ask *directly* for what you want. You will be pleasantly surprised how often you get what you ask for.

I have overheard men accuse a woman of complaining when I know she is not complaining. In conversations among themselves, women may describe problems just to vent, or to make conversation, or to get support. Men misinterpret this type of conversation as complaining. If a man starts giving you suggestions or looks annoyed when you are just discussing or describing a problem, then it is safe to say that he thinks you are complaining. Either change the subject or set him straight. Defuse this potentially troublesome miscommunication immediately.

## Act Like the Competent Professional You Are, Not the Stereotype of a Businesswoman

Julius, VP in a large manufacturing company, asked me:

> Why is it that male executives come in the full spectrum
> of personalities but female executives don't? Most of
> them are so formal and stiff.

Female executives do come in the full spectrum of personalities, but many women are afraid to let their personalities show. You don't have to be glum to be taken seriously.

Men use humor in business more comfortably than women. I thought about this rule while at a symposium in Philadelphia given by the World Affairs Council titled "Can Philadelphia Compete in the World Economy?" The moderator began this serious meeting by telling ten minutes of jokes like a stand-up comedian. He then introduced each speaker with one sentence. The audience loved him. I turned to a friend and asked if she could imagine a woman moderating that panel the same way. Unfortunately, she couldn't—nor could I. What a shame.

Too often women mistake *understanding* the way the men play the game with trying to play it just like a man. Women make poor imitation men. Don't try to act just like a man.

In any game, you play the position that best suits *your* talents. If you are five feet tall, basketball is not your game, but perhaps you will excel at gymnastics. If you are playing football and you are quick, agile, and can throw the football, you don't aim to be a linebacker. Do what *you* do best.

So act like the person you are. Let your competence and strengths shine. Don't act hard because you think that is how a businesswoman should act. You don't have to be overly formal. Don't conceal your sense of humor. You'll need it. You can play by the rules and win by accenting and using your strengths.

## SUMMARY

RULE 2: ACT STRONG.

1. Always try to take control and be in control.

2. Do not be obviously dependent on a superior.

3. Do not let your opponent know he has "gotten to you," even if he has.

4. Do not sulk or complain if things do not go your way.

5. Act like the competent professional you are, not the stereotype of a businesswoman.

# Rule 3:
# Keep Playing to Win
# Even When the Game
# Is No Longer Fun

Whenever I think of this rule, I remember a race on a cold, rainy day in December. I was wearing so many clothes, I looked like a marshmallow. We could barely see through the driving rain. There we were, wet, cold, and shivering, when one of my crewmembers turned to me and said, "Why are we doing this?" The whole crew began laughing. Why, indeed? It certainly wasn't fun. But we knew why we were doing it: We were racing.

There are parts of every competitive sport that are not fun. Think about football, hockey, skiing, running, boxing. Does a runner after a marathon or a boxer after a fight look as if he had a good time? Dealing well with adversity is part of the definition of a good teammate. The person you want on your team is the person who will stick it out in the bad times, someone you can count on through thick and thin.

When you are competing, the goal of the game is to win. If

you are indignant because the required work is too painful or time-consuming, you cannot expect to win. Consider the time and energy Olympic athletes put into practicing their games. If you want to compete in the Olympics of the workplace, you have to face the unpleasant tasks as well as the pleasant ones. Enjoying yourself all the time is wonderful, but enjoyment is an extra bonus. The pleasure that is guaranteed is the sense of accomplishment you get for doing a good job.

The best way to face an odious but necessary task is to focus on your goal and find something positive in the task. "The good thing about working all night is that I get to see the sunrise." Engage your sense of humor and creativity. There is always a positive way to look at adversity. If nothing else, adversity provides you with the opportunity to feel satisfied with yourself when you conquer it.

## Long Hours May Be Part of the Job

Most men dislike long hours but they don't find long hours as stressful as women do. Long hours are "just part of the job." Sam, an engineering consultant, said it bluntly: "Work is a necessary part of my life, and if it takes a lot of hours, that's just the way it is." Tanya, another consultant, observed that the men she worked with considered missing lunch a badge of honor, while she just got hungry. Tanya plans to write a book someday entitled *Real Consultants Don't Eat Lunch.*

Men are more comfortable with working long hours than women for a number of reasons. Men have role models in this area; women don't. Many saw their fathers work long hours. Movie and TV heroes (mostly male) burn the midnight oil in order to crack a case. Working long hours thus becomes part of the definition of what it means to be a man. Working hard also gives many men a sense of accomplishment: it is proof of how much they love and are willing to sacrifice for their families. For men, the social stigma of not supporting their families at whatever income level they consider necessary is stronger than the negative consequences of long hours.

Society is presenting women with an untenable double standard about long hours, an issue brought to light during our national obsession with the O.J. Simpson trial. At the time of the proceedings, the prosecutor, Marcia Clark, was in the midst of a divorce. Her husband sued for custody of the children, citing her long hours working on the case as the reason. At the same time the House of Representatives was considering legislation that would take women with children off welfare if they did not get a job after two years. If you feel conflicted, it is because society is sending you a conflicting message. The norms are in flux. You have to find your personal answer inside yourself.

Some corporate cultures demand long hours. To advance in these companies, you must be willing to work those hours. If you are unhappy, ask yourself why you are working in this kind of environment. If it's not what you want to do, get out. There are better alternatives.

What if you want the rewards, both financial and intellectual, that only working long hours can get you? Adjust your life to make it as comfortable as possible. Try to adapt your social life to your schedule. If events start while you are still working, don't hesitate to show up late. Or don't make a habit of always going straight home. Why not meet a friend who is also working late? Stop at a restaurant regularly for dinner or a snack if you're on your own. You may meet other diners with similar schedules and/or become friendly with the staff.

Although most wives work today, our culture still promotes the picture of a husband working while his wife stays home and cares for the house as the cultural norm. We may disagree intellectually, but this image still has a powerful emotional pull. How many times have you heard a woman joke about needing a wife? It's no joke; you really need one. One of the reasons working long hours is easier for men is because many of them do, in fact, have wives.

In *The Second Shift*,[1] Arlie Hochschild, a sociology professor at the University of California at Berkeley, reported the painful results of her study of two-career families. She found that even in two-career households, only 20 percent of the men shared the housework equally; 70 percent did less than half, but more than a third, of the housework and child care; and 10 percent did less than one third. When men do housework or child care, they see themselves as "helping their wives" or "baby-sitting" their children. Even in the most equitable of families, Hochschild found that the wives still did two thirds of the daily housekeeping jobs and felt responsible for the home and children.

You can't work long hours if you carry the primary responsibility for the housework. If your partner helps, but you have to remind him to do his jobs, you still have primary responsibility. The positive note in Hochschild's study is that men are now doing some of the housework. They are slowly getting the message. Stick to your guns—the only fair split is fifty-fifty. Mowing the lawn once a week or fixing something when it breaks is not the same as being responsible for the never-ending task of housework. This is difficult reeducation for men. Be sensitive, but be firm.

There are only so many hours in a day. Sometimes you have to choose between home responsibilities and work. When forced to make that choice, men choose to limit their time at home while women choose to limit their work hours. Keep a log of how you spend your time for a week or two. Are you dividing the hours the way you really want to?

Single men don't feel the same cultural pressure to keep a neat house or do the cooking as single women do. Men are used to leaving the cooking and cleaning to someone else. They are untroubled about using maids and cooks and eating most meals out. Most women feel guilty. In a recent women's group, everyone acknowledged they knew how Ruth felt when she confessed, "I have to get home early tonight; the house-cleaners are coming tomorrow and I want to straighten up first."

It's hard to ignore a lifetime of training that teaches that housework is the woman's job. This expectation hasn't completely disappeared. When you walk into Jim and Judy's neatly kept house, do you think, "Jim is a great housekeeper. I wonder how he finds the time?"

Can you decrease the hours you spend on household chores? Do you need a housekeeper, a cook, more child care? Does the idea of hiring someone to do these "housewifely chores" make you feel guilty? Are you overzealous about how neat you want your house? You may have to reduce your standards. Fight the cultural expectation that you can do it all. You can't. Super-woman only exists in comic books.

If you don't want to work long hours, you have several choices. First of all, try to work smarter. I'll give you some suggestions how in Chapter Thirteen. The more efficient you are, the fewer hours you have to work. Another option is to find a career or employer that requires more moderate hours. A more unorthodox choice could be to pursue a career that demands long hours, as long as you realize and accept the fact that your opportunities for advancement will be limited because you will not work that many hours. The trade-off of doing work you enjoy and having the free time you want may be worth the price of limited advancement.

The business world can be an endless contest of constant striving for more money, more prestige. Decide how much money and prestige are enough for you. Don't be trapped by society's definition of success; create your own. Choose the kind and quality of life you want.

Long hours always take a toll. Be honest with yourself about your goals and your values. Be sure the goals you are striving for are *your* goals, not a stereotype you are blindly following. Decide what is important to *you* and try to create a work life that will achieve this. Remember, you can define success any way you want. Set your own goals and go after them.

## Getting Clients or Generating Business Can Be as Much a Part of the Job as the Job

Some women talk of getting business so disparagingly that it sounds as if it is an immoral act. It isn't. Julius, a lawyer, puts it simply:

> I know there are things I need to do to get and keep clients. I don't always like to do them, but I do them anyway. Developing a clientele is the name of the game.

Before you can provide your service, somebody has to buy it. It doesn't matter how skilled you are if nobody hires you. From a company's perspective, an employee who can bring business to the firm is more valuable than an equally skilled employee who cannot. Many women are uncomfortable cultivating clients because they feel uncomfortable exchanging services for money. Because women are trained to be caretakers, charging someone for your caretaking feels wrong. Boys are not encouraged to be caretakers. As children, boys trade rather than give away favors. They learn to expect to get something in return for their services. Some men are more comfortable asking for business than others, but selling, rather than giving away, services is more familiar to all of them.

Otto, a senior partner in a large engineering firm, admits that an engineer's ability to cultivate a loyal following is one of the criteria he uses in deciding who will make partner. He thinks women make very good workers but hold themselves back by not developing business. His explanation:

> Women don't understand that they have to contact the people they do business with—the bankers, the suppliers. You have to take them to dinner, take them out to play golf, take them to play tennis. You just have to do it. My female employees get very uptight about that. I tell them that if you're uncomfortable, you don't have to go out for dinner and drinks. Take them to the ball game. Take them to a show. Just take them out.

If you have a good service to deliver and are delivering it efficiently, why take them out? Otto's answer was blunt: because they expect it. If you don't take them out, they will give their business to someone who does.

Going to a ball game with someone I dislike sounds like a trial to me. I wondered if Otto minded spending time with people he didn't like. His response:

> I don't mind it because generally when you are doing business with someone, you have some kind of relation-

ship with them. I normally won't take somebody out I really dislike. But I probably wouldn't do business with him either.

Whenever possible, men prefer to do business with people they like, people they consider friends. One of the keys to getting business is making a lot of the right kind of friends. This is not as daunting as it sounds. When it comes to the workplace, men use a broad definition of "friend." They don't reserve the word "friend" for intimate companions. A friend is someone toward whom you feel friendly. A friend can be a man's longtime confidant, someone with whom he went to school twenty years ago, a country-club member with whom he golfs occasionally, or a friend of his next-door neighbor. Substitute "an acquaintance with whom you have shared some activity" for the male use of the word "friend."

Cultivating business means spending time and energy meeting people. It can mean doing things that are time-consuming and unpleasant. Women are less tolerant than men about associating with people they don't like. Women expect more from their relationships. It will be easier to make the social contacts necessary to get business if you adapt your expectations to the situation.

If you want to cultivate business, you have to do more than just attend events or silently entertain clients. Your prospective clients have to know what you do and think you are good at it. You have to make yourself visible. You have to blow your own horn. June shared her experience:

My husband and I are both lawyers and we both belong to the same church. But when members of our congregation need legal assistance, they ask Barry, my husband, not me. At first I thought this was pure sexism, but there is more to it. I realized that Barry talks about his work in social situations while I usually talk about my personal life.

As an experiment, I began telling anecdotes from my work rather than home in church groups. Guess who got the next referral?

Is developing business always an unpleasant and difficult task? Not if you ask Elaine, a successful "rainmaker"—as lawyers who bring in business are called. Elaine says rainmaking is a snap if you keep these four simple objectives in mind:

1. People have to know and like you.
2. People have to know what you do.
3. People have to know you are expert at what you do.
4. People have to know you want their business.

Find creative ways to meet these goals that are not disruptive to your life. Just letting your neighbors know what you can do can be effective. Even the groups you belong to now, like church or school groups, may be fertile grounds for referrals. Some women worry that they are taking advantage of friends this way. You should look at it like you are really doing your friends a favor. They may need your service but not know where to turn. Wouldn't you prefer to do business with someone you know rather than go to a stranger?

Saul, another successful rainmaker, told me the secret of his success:

I keep my name in the front of people's minds just by being polite and responsive. When people know what you do and feel good about you, they send you business.

Saul always answers clients' calls promptly. He phones present and potential clients periodically, letting them know whenever there is a new legal development that may interest them. He keeps an extensive file of birthdays, anniversaries, children's names, and special interests of people he is cultivating. He sends Christmas cards, birthday cards, and thank-you notes, and writes notes of acknowledgment when he learns of another's accomplishment. If he sees a magazine article that may be of interest to a client, he sends it along with a brief note. These friendly strategies accomplish Elaine's four objectives with minimal effort.

Only you can decide if you are willing to put in the extra time and effort to cultivate clients. This is an important decision; don't take it lightly. In some companies, you aren't respected if you don't bring in new clients, no matter what else you do. If this is the case in your organization, face it. Rather than fight a losing battle, change jobs. If you can't, reconcile yourself to the lowered status and don't take it personally.

Not all companies are inflexible. You may be able to create another track to the top. Try to convince your employer that you are contributing something unique, something else as valuable as bringing in new customers. Develop a niche no one else can fill. Make sure your company appreciates the importance of this niche.

## There May Be Times When It Is Best to Stretch the Truth or to Lie

I think of myself as an honest person, so I was taken aback when Candy, a builder, told me:

The most important thing I learned in your group is to lie a little. Men do it all the time.

I felt better when she gave this example:

We were behind deadline on a renovation when I realized the plans the architect sent just wouldn't work. I asked him to make the needed changes immediately. I tried to be tactful by explaining that although the plan looked good on paper, it was impractical given our time frame. He responded by asking if I was telling him that the plan he submitted was not adequate. Foolish me. I said yes.

The next day he faxed me a copy of an angry letter to my supervisor calling me difficult and unprofessional. Harry, my supervisor, reassured me that my analysis was correct and that I had done nothing wrong.

Then I read Harry's response to the architect. Harry wrote that although the plans were excellent, the owner insisted they be changed. This wasn't true. When I confronted him about his response, he told me that lying to soothe the architect was just good business.

Situations like these are hard to assess. Which was more important, being completely honest and stalling the project, or lying and getting the job done? There are times when you simply can't get the job done if you are completely honest. Only you can decide the priorities.

In business, there are occasions when outright lying will get you the best, or only, result. Luckily, most of the time stretching or shading the truth is enough. And there is a big difference between self-serving manipulative deceit and coloring the truth to make a difficult statement easier to swallow.

Everyone tells white lies, even the most honest person; we're just not supposed to admit it. We teach children that it is always best to tell the truth. But leaders in the mental-health field don't agree with this practice. They have discovered that little white lies can be beneficial to our health.

Dr. Aaron Beck, one of the most respected psychiatrists alive today, stresses in his book *Love Is Not Enough* that complete honesty at all times is harmful, even in the closest of relationships. There are times when cruelty masquerades as honesty. The naked truth can be destructive.

You don't have to tell all the truth all of the time. Giving too much information under the guise of honesty can be self-defeating. Don't confuse being honest with being direct. How much information should you include in your answer? In most cases, the minimal amount necessary to answer the question is sufficient. Simple, direct answers are preferable in most business conversations. You don't have to reveal all your inner thoughts or feelings about the matter.

You could be completely truthful and answer the question "How are you doing on the Smith report?" with "I hate the subject. It's really hard and I don't have nearly enough time to complete it." But you will gain a lot more respect by swallowing hard and saying "It will be done on Wednesday." Complete it by Wednesday and you have told the truth. Your answer wasn't precisely true, but is it lying? You answered the real, underlying question, rather than the specific words.

Your supervisor needs a report and asks, "Do you know how to do this?" If you've never seen that kind of report before, what should you say? Would yes be a lie? The question your supervisor is really asking is "Can you get this done?" If you know that you can look it up and produce the required report, answering yes is the correct answer to the real question.

What does saying yes accomplish? Your supervisor feels calmer, the report is completed, and you look as competent as you really are. What would the completely honest answer, "I don't know how to do it," accomplish? Your supervisor feels unsure of your ability and you look like a novice. He may give the report to someone else and you will miss an opportunity to learn something new. Your supervisor doesn't care what you do to write this report; he just wants it done.

A question like "Have you finished the Jones analysis?" raises similar issues. If it's unfinished but you know that you can do it immediately, should you tell the truth and say no? Your boss will respect your honesty but think you are an inadequate worker. Responding "My secretary has it; I'll have it on your desk in the morning" will preserve your boss's respect for you and let him get a good night's sleep.

Negotiations require even more complex judgments. Your business adversary asks, "Do you have the authority to make this decision?" If you don't, answering truthfully might not get your client the best result. What if your opponent is not budging because he considers you a lightweight and plans to run over you? If you admit that you don't have the power to make a decision, you compound the problem. Answering yes will force him to respect you more, clearly benefiting your client. Just don't make any promises without checking with your client.

You have a different dilemma if you do have the authority to make the decision. Sometimes you can get a better settlement if the negotiation takes longer, or if your opponent thinks you are willing to give in but your client is being unreasonable. Is it better to tell the truth and get your client a poor settlement, or pretend you can't make any decisions without approval and get a better one?

Men and women have different definitions of morality. Not deceiving anyone is an important part of the female moral code.

In male morality, the most important thing is accomplishing what has to be done. To a woman, a lie is a lie. But to men, if a lie is the only way to achieve a necessary result, it's okay. As a woman, you need to find the right balance for you. Don't do anything that makes you hate yourself, but don't sacrifice yourself in the name of being honest.

---

## SUMMARY

RULE 3: KEEP PLAYING TO WIN EVEN WHEN THE GAME IS NO LONGER FUN.

1. Long hours may be part of the job.

2. Getting clients or generating business can be as much a part of the job as the job.

3. There may be times when it is best to stretch the truth or to lie.

# Rule 4:
# Don't Get Emotionally Involved While Playing the Game

Larry, an advertising VP, complained:

> You can't yell at a woman the way you can a man. They are more sensitive. You have to know how to handle them.

How many times have you heard a man groan, "Women; they're too emotional"? I asked Larry how men feel when he yells at them. "I don't know how a man feels," he replied. "I don't even think about it."

I don't like Larry's attitude, but unfortunately it is a typical one. Men pride themselves on being what they think is the opposite of emotional: logical. As children, boys develop their identity by being as different from their mothers as possible—including denying any soft, empathetic feelings.

Little boys learn to hide their emotions. "Keeping a stiff upper lip" becomes an important goal. "Act like a man" doesn't mean "be mature." It really means "hide your emotions."

More from my interview with Larry:

> Women talk to other women about their feelings. Chances are if I upset a woman, my secretary will come in and ask, "Why did you treat her that way?" With a man, chances are 99.9 percent that no one else will know if he is upset. He wouldn't want anyone to know he was criticized.

Logical thinking and emotion are not incompatible. In fact, they complement each other. But men think they are mutually exclusive. Because men have so little experience with emotion, they are often less rational when they are emotional. It's not so for women, but when a man sees a woman showing emotion, he assumes she will not act logically.

There are times when your emotional responses can be detrimental to your business sense. We all have had a personal experience when our heart overruled our head, and we paid for it. This can happen in business, too. Don't ignore your emotions—just be clear that they are complementing, not clouding, your judgment.

Being sensitive, empathetic, and responsive to others' emotions are one of women's strengths. Numerous studies of the effectiveness of female management styles document this. In the male management style, emotions are unnecessary distractions. In the female management style, they are valuable clues. So appreciate your emotions, but don't always let them show. Don't deny yourself the benefits of your strengths, but do take into account the way men may interpret your behavior.

# Don't Take Comments Made by Opponents or Colleagues Personally

Andre, VP for marketing in a major corporation:

> Women are more sensitive, no doubt about that. If I call a man in here and tell him he did something wrong, it's not a major thing. No one likes being criticized—some of the men even argue with me—but it's over in ten minutes. But the women! Sometimes they cry. Sometimes they get so upset they can't function for a few days.

I learned about taking criticism while sailing with Rex, a well-liked and highly respected skipper. As a novice racer, I asked Rex for a crew position on his boat. I expected him to ask about my sailing ability. Instead he responded, "Can you take abuse?" I thought he was joking, but I soon learned otherwise.

In the heat of competition, some skippers yell at other boats and at their crew. Skippers who are aggressive with their opponents are often as aggressive with their own crew. Rex becomes extraordinarily abusive when caught up in the heat of competition. He mentions his reaction to all his prospective crew because he wants to be sure no one on his boat will take his abuse personally.

To sail comfortably with Rex, you have to be able to forget his insults the moment you cross the finish line. Rex is respected not only for his sailing ability, but also for his creativity in stringing together unprintable epithets. I learned from Rex how to disregard insults said in the heat of passion and react with a sense of humor rather than rancor.

No one, including me, is above losing their temper and saying something they regret later. Since sailing with Rex, I always remind my own crew that anything insulting said during a race is forgotten when we cross the finish line.

Helmut, an accountant, voiced another theme I hear often:

> Women are paranoid. They interpret everything that happens to them as happening to them because they are women.

Given the situations women encounter, it's hard *not* to be paranoid! But there is some truth in what Helmut is saying. In my groups, I hear many examples of women misinterpreting behavior and taking remarks as personal affronts when they were being treated the same way any male opponent would be treated. This is because they don't understand the rules.

You have to learn when to take comments or affronts personally while playing the game. You have to consider them in the context of the game. Testing, sparring, and sometimes yelling are part of the game. When dealing with an abusive manager, keep in mind that he may be attacking, but he may not be attacking you. He may be attacking the character playing your position in the game.

There is nothing pleasant about being criticized or insulted. The best thing to do would be to avoid working with abusive men. But if you want to be able to function in an environment that allows this abuse—as I did on Rex's boat—you have to learn to shake these insults off.

Sometimes the anger you encounter has nothing to do with your work or with you. Some men feel a generalized anger at women for invading "male space." Because men develop their identity as men by doing male things, it is important for them to have activities and places clearly defined as male. Your presence in the workplace disrupts this sense of identity. These men are unaware of or unable to articulate the reason for this anger. If you find yourself obligated to work with a man like this, don't bother trying to change him. He will need a therapist for that. Keep reminding yourself that this rage has nothing to do with you. If you can't stop him or get away from him, at least understanding the reason for his abuse will insulate you from the impact of his insults.

## Don't Become Too Attached to Your Clients or Your Goals

Mark, a partner in a large law firm, says:

> I think the biggest problem women lawyers have, especially in negotiations, is keeping their objectivity. Sometimes they fight for their clients like a mother bear fights for her cubs. They become unwilling to back down, even when it would benefit their clients.

The female tendency to care about and nurture relationships is one of women's greatest strengths. But it is also a potential weakness. Its drawback is that too close an attachment to a client or a position can result in a loss of objectivity. I have seen women fight to the death when they would have sustained only a few scratches had they been willing to yield.

I am not suggesting that you be unsympathetic or uncaring; I am suggesting you monitor your feelings for your clients and positions. Use your empathy as a valuable tool, but don't lose sight of your role—that of an objective counselor. If your client is a friend, put that friendship aside during your business relationship. You can resume the friendship later. You will see the case more clearly and do a much better job if you keep some emotional detachment.

You need this detachment to evaluate your position and your client accurately. Too close an attachment will distort your ability to evaluate a position. It will make it harder to recognize when your client is wrong. It will make it more difficult to know when to compromise and when to yield. Your client can ultimately lose because of your lack of objectivity.

Emotional involvement is an easy tendency to exploit. An opponent will try to get you to focus on an emotional but minor point in a negotiation. He hopes you become so attached to it that to win that issue, you yield on a less emotional but more important one.

If you suspect that you are too emotional about an issue, talk to a friend you trust. Get an objective opinion. Struggle to keep an open mind. It is hard to hear advice about an emotional position dispassionately. If someone accuses you of being too attached to a client or a case, carefully consider this criticism before you dismiss it out of hand.

Your empathy and concern with relationships are your strengths, but don't forget they can also be your vulnerabilities.

## Only Show Anger at Appropriate Times

Dorothy, nursing supervisor at a large hospital:

> When I heard that Dr. Gillis had cursed at my nursing staff again, I was furious. I stormed into his office and told him I would not put up with it. He looked at me

blankly. Then I realized I had not taken the time to check the story. I knew something was wrong, so I apologized and left. Later I learned the problem was with a new intern, also named Gillis.

As a human emotion, anger is useful. It serves to motivate us to action when we think someone is intentionally hurting us. But inappropriate or unfocused anger is a useless emotion. It can cloud your judgment and distract you from the task at hand. Dorothy's desire to protect her nurses was admirable but her hotheaded response only caused her embarrassment. Rather than remedy the situation, she created a new problem by raging at the wrong Dr. Gillis.

Women are at a disadvantage when they get angry, especially if they raise their voices. When a man yells, everyone says, "He must be angry." If a woman yells, they say, "She is hysterical." Before you let your anger show, consider the results this will have. Will looking angry get you what you want or will it only hurt your image? When in doubt, take the time to cool off.

Some adversaries will purposely attempt to get you angry, hoping to make you look "weak" or "overemotional." You will find it easier to stay calm if you understand that your opponent's goal is to get you angry and flustered. Don't give him the satisfaction.

So, are women allowed to get angry at all? "Yes," answered Lucy, owner of a successful accounting firm, "women can get angry, but only in very civilized ways. I try to speak quietly, slowly, and deliberately. It's preferable to show too little emotion rather than too much." Lucy went on to extol the advantages of showing anger very sparingly. "If they think you are someone who never gets angry, when you do get angry, they really pay attention."

When is it appropriate to show anger? Only when you think you have something to gain by it.

## SUMMARY

Rule 4: Don't get emotionally involved while playing the game.

1.  Don't take comments made by opponents or colleagues personally.

2.  Don't become too attached to your clients or your goals.

3.  Only show anger at appropriate times.

## CHAPTER EIGHT

# Rule 5:
# Being Aggressive Is Part
# of the Game

*Snakes and snails and puppydog tails, that's what little boys are
    made of.*
*Sugar and spice and everything nice, that's what little girls are
    made of.*

Our culture demands that men be aggressive. Aggression is one
of the elements our culture uses to differentiate male from female. By definition, men's games have to be aggressive. If you
want to play a man's game, you have to be aggressive, too.

The word "aggressive" has a negative connotation for most
women. As a therapist, I used to encourage women to be "assertive," not "aggressive." But not anymore. I have come to realize there are positive as well as negative aspects to aggression.
Aggressive can mean "hostile" or "contentious," but it can also
mean "forceful," "determined," "forward," and "bold." I am not
going to encourage you to be hostile or contentious. These behaviors will get you nowhere. But I am going to encourage you to
be forceful, determined, forward, and bold.

## Choose the Team You Want to Play On and Work to Be Picked for That Team

Lucy, project manager for a large marketing firm:

> I came to this firm because Al was here. He is one of the best consultants around and I wanted to work for him. He never chose me to be on his team. When I complained about this to Sy, a coworker, Sy said simply, "Ask him." I did. Now Al is one of my mentors.

Don't wait to be chosen! Don't be the equivalent of a wallflower at work. Just as many women wait for men to ask them out on dates, most women feel as if they have to wait to be asked to join a team or to be assigned a project. Men lobby to get the attention of the men with whom they want to work. In business, they expect women to do the same.

The dating mores for women are changing. Women are becoming more comfortable asking men out. And men like it. Use these same mores at work. Don't stand by and hope that the person with whom you want to work will choose you. He may not even know you are interested. Tell him you are.

When you ask someone if you can work with him, he may say no. Is fear of rejection holding you back? If it is, remind yourself that no one ever died of rejection. The word "rejection" calls up negative emotions, but work to keep the situation in perspective. Did he reject you as a human being or did he simply say he doesn't need you on his team right now? Did he have room on his team for you? Could he have wanted someone with different skills? Remember, if he says no, you have lost nothing. The benefits of letting him know you want to work for him far outweigh any momentary bad feelings you may have if he says no.

The tenet "It's not what you know, it's who you know" holds true in the office. The first action that a man who wants to get ahead takes is to find a friend or mentor who will help him get there. The men I talked to said they looked around their office and figured out whom they wanted to work with. Then they did whatever was necessary to be visible and get that person's attention.

Think about the kind of work you want to do and find out who does that kind of work. Determine who you would like to work for and get his attention. Figure out who you should be allied with and make that alliance. Be direct and clear.

Many of the successful men and women I interviewed told me they were interested in mentoring women, but no woman asked them. Don't wait for someone to approach you. Choose who you would like to be your mentor and let him or her know it. The mentoring relationship is a special one in which people have to "click." It is particularly important, though, that as a woman, you make sure that any potential male mentor knows that your interest in him is work-related.

Some men will think that your interest is social. So don't just be clear, be blatant. In a perfect world this wouldn't be necessary, but ours is not a perfect world. Until you are sure he knows your interest is work-related, keep personal conversations to a minimum, try to meet in the office rather than in informal settings like lunch, and steer any conversations that wander away from work back to business. It's worth the effort to be alert and maybe even a bit stiff at first to avoid potential misunderstandings. Once you are sure of your relationship, you can relax.

## Make Yourself Visible

Karen, an art director for an insurance company:

> I didn't understand what was happening. I loved work-
> ing for Gerry. He often told me my work was excellent.
> I worked late several nights a week and he was always
> appreciative of the product I produced. I thought he
> was my mentor and that I was going places. But when a
> position opened that I thought was perfect for me, I
> didn't get it. Gerry said he was surprised that I wasn't
> promoted.
>
> But three months later Gerry was promoted. Only
> then did I learn that Gerry had been taking credit for my
> work. Gerry wanted me to go with him, but I decided to
> let him do his own work.

Karen learned too late the biggest pitfall of not being visible.
Someone else can take credit for your work. Because she did not
make herself more visible in the company, no one other than
Gerry knew of her skill. Unfortunately, Karen's experience is not
uncommon. Some men, like Gerry, are aware of women's pro-
pensity for anonymity and take advantage of it.

Many women feel that they do wonderful work, but nobody appreciates them or rewards them for it. Unfortunately,
this is true. Women are taught that if you humbly do good
work you will be rewarded. Wrong! If the good work is all done
behind the scenes but you never tell anyone how good the work
is, you will not be rewarded because no one *knows* that you've
done it.

Assuming someone will know you are a good worker just because you are a good worker is an oft-made mistake. Your work

has to be noticed in order to be judged. Never assume anyone is aware of how much work you did or how hard you worked on a particular project. Your supervisor may be too busy or too self-absorbed to notice—or he may be taking credit for it himself. If you want your good work to be recognized, you have to call attention to it.

I often hear stories about incompetent men in high places. If you are wondering how some man you consider incompetent is so successful and so well regarded by his superiors, look around. He probably has several women subordinates behind him doing all the work, politely waiting to be rewarded.

Bragging is a part of the male culture. If you are like most women, bragging feels impolite and unnecessary to you, but it is important for you to recognize the function of bragging. Women expect others to be aware of how hard they work because women are very aware of what the people around them are doing. Men expect others not to notice their work because men focus more narrowly on what they are doing and don't notice what others are doing. Men brag because they are convinced that no one will notice them otherwise. If you don't learn to call attention to yourself in a male system, you run the risk of being invisible.

It isn't necessary to brag in the same way men do; I would even caution against it. When women brag like men, it looks wrong to men and can backfire. But do make sure that your successes are apparent. Quietly and politely insist that your accomplishments be recognized. If you just sit in the back room and get the job done, no matter how splendid the job, you won't get anywhere. Talk about your successes. Display your work. You will not advance if you sit passively by and wait to be discovered. Show off your good work; you deserve the credit.

## Ask for Interesting Work

Marty, an insurance executive, told me this story. He asked if I could explain Sylvia's behavior.

> Sylvia is one of my assistants. She is very capable and I like her. I thought she knew this. But last week she stopped talking to me. I have no idea why she is angry. When I ask, she just grumbles that I should know. This is what I hate about working with women. Women are a puzzle.

I asked if he had given anybody any raises or awards recently. He said no, but he had recently delegated an exciting assignment to Charlie, another assistant. When I asked if this could be the problem, his response was:

> Of course not! If she had wanted that assignment, she would have asked.

I asked Marty if he was willing to wager an expensive lunch on whether or not Sylvia thinks that assignment should have gone to her. He immediately agreed to the bet. Then we asked Sylvia.

I thoroughly enjoyed the lunch he bought me.

In the business world, men expect you to be aggressive. If you are not, they interpret it as lack of interest. Marty would have given the assignment to Sylvia had she only asked. Since it is difficult enough to get choice assignments, do not get passed over because of misunderstandings like this.

Decide what work you want to do and ask for it. Don't wait for the work to come to you. Be a squeaky wheel, if necessary. In women's circles, this behavior might be considered rude. In the male world, it is just the way the game is played.

## Take Risks

The owner of a large engineering firm explained his attitude about risks:

> I don't mind taking a risk if I weigh it and decide it is worth it. I don't mind making a mistake if I knew it was a risk. No one bats a thousand. You back the wrong horses sometimes.
>
> If you want to advance in your field, you have to take risks.

Men interpret attempting difficult work as a sign of strength and respect you for it. Willingness to undertake difficult tasks is part of the yardstick men use to judge each other. Volunteering for difficult work is a demonstration of strength and bravery. Men respect those who volunteer and belittle those who don't. You must be willing to volunteer for difficult work—preferably visibly.

Men are much less fearful than women about trying something new. Because of the pressure society puts on them to be experts, men learn to "act" competent (see Rule 1). They pretend to be knowledgeable about subjects they know nothing about. They discover that if they try something they have never done before, they just might get it right. Men develop confidence that they can "pull something off." Part of the fun of the game is seeing how much you can get away with.

If you don't fight your fear of taking risks, you are giving some men an opportunity to take advantage of you. They know you will never advance unless you take risks. They have you to do the mundane work, giving them time for more exciting assignments. Allowing a fear of taking risks to dominate you is an invitation for someone to help you become the woman *behind* the man.

Traditionally, men protect women from risks, and it is a situation with which both sexes can feel comfortable. But in business, this protection can be a trap. Don't be deceived by an overly protective mentor. A mentor who allows or encourages you not to take risks is hurting rather than helping you. This is a smothering, not a mentoring, relationship. A real mentor will push you so you can discover the true extent of your abilities.

Being afraid to take risks is caused by a combination of fear of making mistakes and passivity. If you are hesitant to take a risk, remind yourself that if you never try anything difficult, you will never grow. There has to be a first time for everything. Have some confidence in your ability to figure out or to learn to do something you have never done before.

While I was helping my brother move into a new apartment, he inadvertently taught me an important lesson about risk taking. Four of us were helping him carry a very heavy table. As we were lugging it across the room, it suddenly fell apart. Everyone gasped in dismay—except my brother. He began to laugh.

His explanation:

Whenever I see a button, I just have to push it.

My brother had noticed a button on the underside of the table and couldn't resist pushing it. Apparently, this old table was meant to come apart and this button was the release.

I contrasted my brother's reaction to that unknown button to what mine would have been. Because he did not know what the button would do, he pushed it to find out. My response would have been the opposite. Because I did not know what that button would do, I would have been too afraid of causing damage to push it.

When we finished laughing at the table's disintegration, we discovered that it was much easier to move now that it was in separate pieces. From then on, I promised myself that whenever I saw a button, I would push it. I haven't been sorry.

Risk taking usually pays off.

---

## SUMMARY

RULE 5: BEING AGGRESSIVE IS PART OF THE GAME.

1.  Choose the team you want to play on and work to be picked for that team.

2.  Make yourself visible.

3.  Ask for interesting work.

4.  Take risks.

## CHAPTER NINE

# Rule 6:
# Fighting Is Part of the Game

Men enjoy fighting in a way most women don't. Al, a real-estate developer, put it this way:

> I enjoy a good fight. It gives me a chance to flex my mental muscles.

Not all men enjoy fighting as much as Al, but all men do understand that it is part of the game. Have you noticed how often men refer to their profession as a battlefield?

Fighting has a different emotional meaning for men than for women, as an article from *The Wall Street Journal*[1] illustrates. This article reported that a group of highly successful men, the California chapter of the Young Presidents Organization, was about to hold their next meeting at a place called Sky Warriors rather than at their usual retreat. At Sky Warriors, men pilot vintage World War I fighter planes and participate in simulated dogfights, with an instructor onboard to take over if necessary. The organizers chose to hold their meeting at Sky Warriors because "you can't get that kind of bonding over a conference table."

For men, fighting can be a positive experience, bringing them together.

## Fight Fair

Howard, a publishing executive, expresses a common complaint:

> I hate fighting with a woman. Women never know when a fight is over. They don't back down when it is obvious they can't win. Women are so brutal; they go for the jugular every time. I wish they would learn to leave a little blood.

Ted, an insurance executive, offers this comment:

> One of the ugliest sights in the world is two women fighting each other. When a man is involved, at least one of them knows the rules.

How *could* women know how to fight? Our culture teaches them that "nice girls don't fight," and most girls don't. The only guidance most of them are given about fighting is the proverb "All's fair in love and war." No one teaches them that even in war there is a code of honor that all but the very bad guys follow.

Until I began racing sailboats, I never understood what "fair fighting" meant. I thought it was an oxymoron. But I learned that fighting is not the free-for-all I always thought it was. Fair fighting is a formal game with a set of rules to be rigidly followed. Picture a duel:

> At high noon, two cowboys stand back-to-back. The town looks empty, but all the townspeople are peering

anxiously through the windows. The cowboys each take ten measured paces, turn, and shoot.

Why doesn't one of the townspeople shoot the bad guy? Why do the fighters take the ten measured paces instead of shooting after just two?

The most efficient way for one gunfighter to kill another would be to shoot the other in the back without warning. But if he does, he will not earn accolades. He will be considered the lowest kind of lowlife possible because he didn't fight fair.

The goal of a fight is not only to win, but also to display your skill at winning within the rules. Our culture has a long, honored tradition of fair fighting. You can see this in our myths and our movies. Shoot-outs at high noon. Gentlemen slapping each other with gloves and saying, "Choose your weapon." Boxers overcoming hardships to knock out a dishonest adversary.

Before I started racing, I always assumed that in a fight you did whatever was necessary to win. The concept of "not hitting below the belt" was perplexing. In boxing, I know where the belt is, but how do you know where the belt is on a sailboat or in a verbal argument or in business? The men seem to know.

Now that I have been racing awhile, the rules of fair fighting no longer seem mysterious. I learned the rules the same way little boys do—by playing. But there is an easier way. When women ask me to recommend a book on fair fighting, I recommend the Boy Scout Manual. I'm only half joking. A John Wayne movie is just as instructive. You already know the concepts; you just have to translate them into the workplace.

Observe the way the men around you fight. Pay attention to the winners and losers. How long did they stay angry? How are the opponents relating to each other a week after the fight? A month after? Who is respected and who is considered a cheat?

How much blood was spilled? If you keep an open mind, a recognizable pattern will emerge.

You *must* learn to fight fair, and that's what we'll cover in the rest of this chapter. The amount you may win by fighting unfairly will never be worth the damage to your reputation and the loss of potential allies.

## Don't Be Too Passive or Too Aggressive

Have you been criticized for being too passive? Too aggressive? Both? Do you feel as if you can't win—as if you are criticized no matter how you act? Unfortunately, you may be right.

When men consider you too passive, you lose. But when you act aggressive, you may lose just the same. To some men, any aggression by a woman is too much. Even a reasonably aggressive woman looks wrong to men who are not used to women fighting or going after what they want. We have all heard men label women who are acting appropriately "aggressive," "unreasonable," or even "bitchy."

But this masks an important problem. Some women are so inexperienced at fighting that the criticism they receive is appropriate. If you are criticized for being too passive or too aggressive, ask a woman you trust and respect to help you evaluate the criticism. A man may feel more comfortable if you are too passive to be effective in your work. A realistic, objective woman can give you the best feedback.

For most women, the problem is too much passivity, not too much aggression. (For more about overcoming passivity, see Chapter Twelve.) You *must* conquer any passive tendencies. It took a lot of work on my part to overcome my passive traits. But now I feel comfortable being aggressive when it is necessary. It gets easier with practice.

Passivity is easy to recognize, but how do you know if you are too aggressive? Some women are so uncomfortable or unused to any aggression that they go overboard. In an effort to rid themselves of passivity, they eliminate any softness. It is easier to be very aggressive than just aggressive enough.

The optimal amount of aggression for each task is the minimum amount needed to get the job done. A fight in business does not have to be a fight to the death. Leave enough life in your adversaries so that you can work, or play, or fight again tomorrow.

## Find Your Opponent's Achilles' Heel and Go for It

When I wanted to learn to race sailboats, I went to sailboat racing school. I expected to learn the rules and techniques of racing. I did not know I would also learn some lessons about the unwritten rules as well.

Before the start of a sailboat race, boats sail around the starting line, jockeying to get into the best starting position. Because there are so many boats in so little space, the racing rules for starting are very rigid. Certain maneuvers are punishable by penalties that make it almost impossible for the transgressor to win. Part of racing strategy is to try to force your opponent to make one of these maneuvers.

One of my friends in the class, who was racing in another boat, forced my boat to make such a maneuver. I was angry that my so-called friend would do that to me. He knew I was new at racing and vulnerable. When I confronted him after the race, he looked at me as if I were speaking another language. He had no idea why I was angry. He simply said in a puzzled tone, "We were racing." Exploiting my inexperience was part of the game.

Too often women hold back from exploiting someone's vulnerability, or get angry as I did when an opponent capitalizes on theirs. Neither response is effective. Being reluctant to exploit an advantage can cost you the battle. If you are in a competitive situation, anything that allows you to win within the rules is fair. Your opponent's weak spot can be the quickest, most bloodless way to win. Your goal is not to strike out of cruelty, but not to hold back out of kindness either.

If exploiting a weakness is the quickest, fairest, cleanest way to win, go for it.

## Know When to Stop

Although the game's not over until it's over, there is a point at which it's over. Remember, politicians don't wait until the last vote is counted. When the winner is obvious, the loser concedes. You are expected to stop fighting at the point when it is clear you cannot win. And then you are expected to lose gracefully—no anger, no excuses, no tears.

How do you know when it's over?

It's over when it is clear you cannot win. You have to trust your ability to accurately assess when it is time to concede. You have to be specific about your goals. When you know exactly what your goals are, it is easier to recognize when losing is inevitable.

It's over when you decide the cost of winning is too high. You have to be ready to concede a small point as part of a strategy to gain a bigger one. You have to keep your perspective and remember that your goal is to triumph overall, not to win every point.

How do you know when to stop?

- You stop when you have accomplished your objective—when you have won the argument, not annihilated your opponent.
- You stop when it is clear you cannot win.
- You stop when it makes sense to cut your losses.
- You stop when a higher authority, like a referee, tells you to stop.
- You stop when you see that it is to your tactical advantage to lose this battle in order to win the war.

## Let Your Opponent Save Face

I am always amazed at how compassionate men are to each other when they fight. They try to win by doing the least necessary amount of damage to each other. They protect each other's egos. As long as they achieve their objective, they allow the other person to appear as if he gave up willingly.

Allowing your opponent to save face is a very practical way to fight. By allowing your opponent to save face, you:

- Give the person who is losing the choice of giving up now and looking like a winner or being beaten later and looking like a loser. This shortens the battle.
- Increase the likelihood that your opponent will do the same for you if the situation is reversed in a future fight.
- Earn the right to expect a favor in return.
- Reduce the anger level, which eases the way toward being friends after the fight.

- Earn the reputation of being big enough to give the other person a break.

## Be a Gracious Winner and a Good Loser

Winning and losing with style is easier when you think of business as a game. No matter what the outcome of this game, there will be another game tomorrow.

The way your opponent feels when you win or lose will bias the way he treats you in the future. It is to your advantage to leave him feeling as positive as possible. Even though he was an opponent in this game, he may be an ally in the next. Your goal is not only to win, but also to keep your opponents (and teammates) interested in playing with you again.

If you do lose, don't be humorless and unfriendly. Don't complain or sulk. Don't cry. Tears are unacceptable for women, although, ironically, tears are becoming popular for men. When a man cries, he gets points for being strong and sensitive; when a woman cries, she is considered a wimp.

Don't carry a grudge when the battle is over. Remember, when it's over, it's over. Distance yourself enough to appreciate your opponent's skill. Make it a point to congratulate your opponent when you lose.

Being a good winner is every bit as important as being a good loser. Draw attention to your success but be careful not to cross the fine line between making yourself visible and gloating. The hallmark of a good winner is her ability to ensure that everyone knows she is the victor while giving her opponent the room to save face.

When someone gives you a good fight, acknowledge his skill and compliment him. Be certain he knows you think he played a good game. Whether you win or lose, always thank your opponent for playing with you. Let him know you are looking forward to a rematch.

Enjoy your victories and learn from your losses. Remember, there will always be another opportunity to win or lose tomorrow.

---

### SUMMARY

RULE 6: FIGHTING IS PART OF THE GAME.

1. Fight fair.

2. Don't be too passive or too aggressive.

3. Find your opponent's Achilles' heel and go for it.

4. Know when to stop.

5. Let your opponent save face.

6. Be a gracious winner and a good loser.

## CHAPTER TEN

# Rule 7:
# You Are Part of a Team

*Women don't make good team players.*

I heard this complaint from most of the men I interviewed and I agree. At first glance, this presents us with a quandary. Women are better than men at collaborating and cooperating. Why aren't they naturally good teammates? Isn't team playing just cooperating?

Team playing is more than just cooperating. It is a formal way of relating. Team playing has its own set of rules. There are unwritten rules about how you form teams, who is on your team, how you signal which team you are on, and how you treat your teammates.

As children, girls get very little experience playing on teams. They aren't exposed to these unwritten rules. While boys are playing in groups and on teams, girls are playing in pairs. Girls learn about cooperation, but not about team playing.

To be a good team player in business situations, you have to understand what being part of a team means to a man. Teams are an important source of identity for boys. Team playing is the closest boys come to intimacy. To boys, their teams are as important as their family or their country. Preadolescents' "secret" clubs and teenage gangs are examples of this phenomenon.

For women, the trappings of a team seem artificial, but they are very important to men. Women relate to others based on the commonalities and shared feelings they recognize in each other. It is these shared emotional values, often communicated by subtle cues rather than directly verbalized, that are most important to women. Because men have difficulty recognizing unspoken similarities, they have to rely on the more clear-cut signals, like uniforms, that teams have.

Boys and girls develop relationships very differently. Girls form relationships based on shared emotions. They become close by sharing secrets. Boys form relationships based on shared experiences. They become close by striving for the same goals. And it is team playing that provides them with shared experiences and shared goals.

## Teams Wear Uniforms

Audrey, owner of a jewelry boutique, told me this story:

> While having lunch in a restaurant, I admired a man's suspenders and pointed them out to a friend. Then I noticed another man wearing suspenders—and another. My friend reminded me that we were a block from the stock exchange. In Philadelphia [where I come from], the broker uniform is brightly colored suspenders.

Every team, from the U.S. Army to the local Little League, has a uniform. Every sport has its own style of uniform. We distinguish the football player from the hockey player by his style of clothing. And we can tell who is on which hockey team by that team's particular uniform. A uniform can be as elaborate as a fancy suit with badges and epaulets or as simple as a particular color neckerchief. A uniform differentiates friend from foe.

The custom of wearing uniforms migrated from the battlefield and sports contests to the workplace. The uniforms are not as stereotyped in the workplace, but they are recognizable nonetheless. Every profession has its own style of uniform and every organization has its own distinctive variation of this general uniform.

Bankers wear very conservative suits, but some banks may allow a choice in the shirt color. Lawyers wear dark suits, but the lawyers in some law firms wear European designer suits and others wear Brooks Brothers. A particular unit in a large corporation may favor a particular color tie.

Uniforms present a problem for women team members. The traditional uniforms are male. A woman stock trader would look foolish in a two-tone shirt with suspenders. But if you are not wearing some version of your team's uniform, your male coworkers won't feel you are part of the team.

It takes all of a woman's fashion sense and creativity to figure out how to dress. But this problem is not limited to women.

Saul, a successful management consultant, informed me:

> Women complain about how hard it is to dress for business. They think that men do not put any energy into it. But I have to dress differently for each of my accounts. This is my bank outfit. Take note of how I look.

Saul was wearing a dark Brooks Brothers suit with a white shirt. When we met again for lunch the following week, there was my previously conservatively dressed friend in a highly styled designer suit. He had just come from a meeting at an advertising agency. He said:

> My clients do not think twice about my clothes—and that's the point. They just feel comfortable around me. If I looked like this at the bank, I wouldn't be as trusted. By the way, it is not just the suit that makes the difference, it is the details. I pay a lot of attention to getting the details right.

Saul's advice is worth taking. Finding the style of clothing that will make your teammates recognize you as part of the team is important. It can be difficult, but it's not impossible. Saul's advice about details is helpful. Sometimes doing something as simple as carrying a conservative briefcase instead of a purse can make the crucial difference.

Your coworkers won't be able to explain why, but they will feel more comfortable and be able to work better with you if you look like part of the team.

Organizational psychologists have studied how dress affects women's careers. It has a tremendous impact.

Experimenters asked volunteers to rate the competence of women. The experimenters gave all the volunteers the same work samples and showed them pictures of the same women, but they varied the women's clothing.[1] The women wore one of three suits. One was very boring, ugly, and boxy; another attractive and conservative; and the last very shaped and stylish. They asked the volunteers to rate the women's competence by judging samples of their work.

Although all the subjects saw the same work samples, they rated them differently depending on the women's dress. When the women wore the attractive, conservative suits, the raters consistently gave them the highest score. The women dressed in the very stylish suit rated second, and the women in the boring suit scored the lowest of all.

You have to decide how important it is to you to make your colleagues comfortable. I think it is worth the trouble, but it's your decision. Some women have told me angrily that they have dressed to please men all their lives and refuse to do it any longer. I think they are confusing issues. Wearing a uniform is not the same as wearing high heels to please men. High heels serve no function, but uniforms do. Men wear uniforms to identify themselves; why wouldn't they expect their female colleagues to do the same? Uniforms are a signal to others that you are on their team, and not a sign of subservience.

If you are lucky enough to have a female teammate who is accepted, analyze her clothes. You can try to adapt the "flavor" of her clothes to your style. And keep Saul's suggestion about details in mind. Experiment with different styles to see if you observe differences in the way the men treat you. You probably will.

I don't think there is any way around wearing some version of the proper uniform. I am not suggesting you give up your individuality or your independence. But like it or not, your dress can have an effect on your success. Put some thought into finding a style of clothing that is the best marriage of your taste and your team's uniform.

## Teammates Help Each Other

Belinda, a computer programmer, learned this rule by accident:

> I never liked Charles. He's pompous and condescending, so when I saw him struggling with a project due the next day, my first response was to gloat. But then my soft side

got the better of me. I stayed late helping him, the whole time kicking myself for being a pushover.

That Friday, for the first time, the men in my office asked if I wanted to join them for happy hour. They've treated me differently ever since.

In war movies, soldiers carry wounded buddies to safety. In sports movies, the best player skips his anniversary dinner to put in extra time helping the team's poorest player. These are strong cultural images.

Teammates help each other for more than altruistic reasons. Boys learn early on that a team is only as strong as its weakest member. Whenever an individual improves his skills, it benefits the whole team. The better each player is, the better the whole team will be.

If the goal of the game is to win, then helping others, even those you don't like, will help you reach your goal.

Boys learn that they don't have to like someone to play with him. And you don't have to like someone to help him. You help him because you want your *team* to win. There will be instances when you are asked to help someone you don't like. It may be unpleasant, but you have to do it. If you refuse, you will be branded a poor team player. Remember that his improvement benefits you. If you are unwilling to help him, at least make it look as if you tried.

Just as men are reluctant to ask for help, they are very careful in how they give it. Belinda won her colleagues' respect not only because she helped Charles, but also because of the way she helped him: she just sat down with him and started working. Men are concerned with letting each other save face. Charles didn't ask for help, but he visibly put in long hours. When a man sees another man working hard, giving it his all and getting nowhere, he knows his help will be appreciated. Typically, he won't ask if he can help; he just starts doing so—just as Belinda did.

Helping teammates is a part of the game that works to your advantage. Some men may not want to help a woman. Some men may not want to help you. But these same men feel compelled to help a teammate. Some men genuinely want women to perform better; others just want the women they work with to be able to carry their own weight in the team. Either way, these men are willing, sometimes begrudgingly, to extend the tradition of helping to women. You should offer your teammates the same type of aid.

## Always Be Loyal to Your Team

Pete, an attorney, described an embarrassing moment in court:

> My firm and I were being raked over the coals because of a mistake one of my partners made in my absence. I hated being called incompetent and wanted to defend myself by agreeing that my partner handled the situation inadequately. But I knew that I couldn't disparage a partner. If I defended myself by singling out and blaming my partner, I would lose even more respect because everyone would judge me a traitor.

I then asked Pete if he ignored his partner's mistake. "No," he said. "I got him alone and really chewed him out. He won't make that mistake again. But we kept a united front for the court and the rest of the firm."

It is difficult to stick up for your team or for a teammate when he is wrong, but don't underestimate the importance of

this. To men, disloyalty to a teammate is the equivalent of trea-
son. Women tend to evaluate each person on his or her own merits, but men view an insult to any team member as an insult to
the whole team. If you find it impossible to defend a teammate,
at least try to stay neutral in public. Have it out with that teammate in private later.

Don't compromise your values, but do your best to keep up
the appearance of team loyalty.

## The Good of Your Team Comes Before Your Personal Interests

Manuel paid this dubious compliment to a partner in his accounting firm:

> I really respect Frederick. He canceled his vacation with
> his family to prepare for this presentation.

Putting your team first is an old and valued tradition. The whole
is more important than any of its parts. We honor the man who
dies for his country. We respect the player who disqualifies himself so he can be replaced by a better player who can ensure a
victory.

We've all watched this tradition be ignored, but it still stands
as an ideal. There will be times when you refuse to put the good
of your team before your own good or the good of your family.
This is especially true if you have children. Some companies recognize that workers are more productive if they can balance their
lives, but not all of them do. I would never recommend putting
your children second. But you won't get ahead if you buck the

corporate culture. If you want to work in a company like Manuel's, whose culture values work over home, try to make it look as if you are putting the company first. Or try to find a more reasonable place to work.

## Always Give 100 Percent . . . or Make It Look Like You Do

Diane, manager of an insurance company, is renowned for her dedication to her company. She shared one of her secrets with me:

> I come in at seven o'clock every morning. I use the quiet time as soon as I come in to organize my day. Clients are impressed because they see my coat on the rack and my work spread on my desk early in the morning. What they don't realize is that while my coat is on the rack, at eight o'clock my body is upstairs in the gym.

We would all be happier and healthier if we could give 100 percent to everything we do. This is the recipe for a satisfying life. But life is not that simple. Unfortunately, conflicting responsibilities make it an impossible achievement.

Putting 100 percent into work would mean no time for friends, families, social lives, or hobbies. Giving up or greatly curtailing our private lives is unhealthy, both physically and emotionally. Yet the male work ethic puts work first. No matter how effective you are, men respect you less if they think you are not putting all your energies into your work.

Both men and women today acknowledge the need for balance in our lives. We are in a time of transition. Traditionally, men have left their home life to women and just concentrated on their work. While most companies will give lip service to the need for balanced lives, the ethic of giving 100 percent to your team is still operative.

Giving 100 percent is another rule in which appearance can be as important as reality. Diane found a way to keep her reputation and get the exercise she needs. Look at the dedicated workers in your company. Some are really sacrificing their personal lives for the good of the team, but others are staying late in the office doing personal tasks like paying bills.

Giving 100 percent is a part of team playing that is deeply embedded in men's sense of morality. You do irreparable damage to yourself if it looks like your other interests and responsibilities are more important. It isn't necessary to neglect the other parts of your life, but it is helpful to keep quiet about them. You don't have to put your work first, but you do have to look like a good teammate who is giving your team 100 percent.

## SUMMARY

RULE 7: YOU ARE PART OF A TEAM.

1. Teams wear uniforms.

2. Teammates help each other.

3. Always be loyal to your team.

4. The good of your team comes before your personal interests.

5. Always give 100 percent . . . or make it look like you do.

# PART THREE

# FACING AND OVERCOMING SELF-DEFEATING BEHAVIORS

# Introduction

When I asked the men I interviewed for their most frequent complaints about their female colleagues, I expected their answers to reflect male prejudice about women, not real problems. As I expected, some responses were unwarranted and unreasonable, but not all. The men consistently described the same self-defeating patterns I often observed in my groups for businesswomen: passivity, disorganization, and a fear of making mistakes.

I then asked successful businesswomen for their complaints about their female colleagues. The businesswomen echoed the men's complaints, pointing out the same self-defeating behaviors. They then talked to me about how they overcame these problems.

As a therapist, I commonly help women to overcome problems like fear of mistakes, passivity, and difficulty prioritizing. In the next three chapters, I will explain why and how these behaviors are self-defeating. Each chapter is a kind of minimanual on how to conquer an unwanted self-defeating behavior. I'll give you the tools you need to evaluate yourself honestly and determine if any of these behaviors is a problem for you. If you are hampered by self-defeating behaviors, I will teach you how to use the latest, most effective psychological techniques to change them.

We all have strengths and weaknesses. If you recognize any of these behaviors in yourself, and if you are like most of us, you will, don't berate yourself. If you were perfect, you wouldn't be human. The purpose of these chapters is to help you eliminate the behaviors you don't want and replace them with more effective ways of working. A theme you will encounter often in the next three chapters is worth stating now: punishing yourself does not help you change behavior; it only makes you feel bad. Reward yourself for positive change. Give yourself credit for having the courage and integrity to take on the challenge of personal growth.

## CHAPTER ELEVEN

# Changing Your Attitudes Toward Mistakes

The most devastating of the self-defeating behaviors is fear of making mistakes. This is really the same as fear of failure. I can't stress this enough: *It is essential that you learn to make mistakes comfortably.* It is essential that you risk failing. Changing this self-defeating behavior will change your life more than any other change I will suggest.

Answer these questions as honestly as you can.

> Do you ever make mistakes?
> Have you made any in the last three months?
> If you remember any, describe one.
> What do you do if you make a mistake?
> What do you do if your mistake is irrevocable?

Everyone makes mistakes, but the way you deal with mistakes separates the winners from the losers. Compare your answers for the above with those below, from a very successful male attorney.

> AM: Do you ever make mistakes?
> John: Of course, everyone makes mistakes.

AM:   Have you made any in the last three months?

John:   Sure.

AM:   Would you tell me one?

John:   (long pause)

He couldn't remember any. I ran into him a few weeks later at a party. He came running across the room just to tell me that he had been thinking about my questions about mistakes, and he remembered one. *One!* How many can you remember? We'll address this lawyer's response later. For now, let's keep comparing.

AM:   What do you do if you make a mistake?

John:   I fix it.

AM:   What if you can't?

John:   I ask someone more experienced for help in fixing it.

AM:   What if it can't be fixed?

John:   I feel bad.

AM:   For how long?

John:   A long time. Sometimes even a day and a half.

Most of the men I interviewed answered this question with "a day and a half." It seems to be the magic number.

My female friends and I developed a running joke about this intriguing fact. Whenever anyone makes a mistake, we encourage each other to remember it for a day and a half. If I tell a friend about a mistake I made yesterday, rather than being sympathetic, she is likely to respond, "You still have half a day to think about it." If no one is around to say this to me, I say it to myself. It gives me a chuckle and helps to take the sting out of the mistake.

The men I interviewed said that they were appalled by the way they have seen women deal with mistakes. A vice-president of a large insurance company gave his opinion:

> Women get stuck on mistakes. Women remember them, ruminate about them, are frozen or devastated by them, brag about them, and don't act for fear of making one.

Unfortunately, this is an accurate description. Research on gender differences shows that, in general, women do have a harder time than men when they err or fail. This difference evolves from the way the two sexes are traditionally raised. Compare the way boys and girls are socialized about mistakes:

> Little boys play a lot of competitive team sports.
> Little girls play dolls.
> Little boys make a lot of mistakes playing team sports.
> Little girls can't make a lot of mistakes playing dolls because there are few or no rules.
> When boys make mistakes, they are encouraged to go back and try harder.
> When girls make mistakes, they are comforted.
> Boys learn that making a mistake may be embarrassing but not fatal.
> Girls learn mistakes are something to feel bad about.
> Boys learn that you earn your team's respect by striving to improve your skills after making a mistake.
> Girls learn you will be consoled if you call attention to your mistakes.

As a child, you did not have many opportunities to learn how to respond to mistakes productively. If you were like most girls, your favorite activities were playing with dolls or role-playing games like house. When you're playing house, you just cannot make enough mistakes from which you can learn. If you did enjoy games of skill, you probably enjoyed more solitary ones, like playing a musical instrument or dancing. You often practiced by yourself, and only showed these skills off when they were perfected. Most of the time no one was with you when you made a mistake. Even if you were a tomboy or had lots of brothers and often played with boys, adults treated you differently from the boys when you made mistakes. Instead of encouraging you to try harder, as they did with the boys when a mistake was made, it is more likely they comforted you, leaving your mistake uncorrected.

Not being encouraged to correct a mistake or try harder leaves girls with a sense that mistakes are irrevocable and a feeling of helplessness. Girls do not get a chance to learn to respond to a mistake with a positive action. They learn to respond with a negative emotion—like disappointment, worry, or self-depreciation.

Listen to Rhonda, co-owner of an architecture firm:

> My partner, Buddy, and I made a big mistake on the city contract. I felt too devastated to do any work. I decided to just go home. Buddy insisted we try to fix it, even though it looked impossible. We stayed up all night and got the contract in just under the wire.

Worrying about, ruminating over, feeling bad about mistakes is a waste of time and energy. It is time and energy that could be much better used in moving on. The only useful way to respond to mistakes is to learn from them. Nobody enjoys making mistakes. But ruminating about them is a waste of time. Learn what you can so you won't make that mistake again, then let it go.

You are going to make mistakes. The more productive you are, the more mistakes you will make. The more risks you take, the more mistakes you will make. Of course, the more productive you are and the more risks you take, the more *successful* you will be.

If a mistake is not worth remembering, it is definitely not worth advertising. The men I interviewed repeatedly told me they were baffled by the way women seemed to "advertise" or "brag about" their mistakes. A comment from Tyrone, an accountant, illustrates this:

> I have always been very impressed by Susan's work. The product she produces is consistently superior. But she tells me about all the mistakes she made that I would never have been aware of. It's as if she wants me to think she's incompetent. It does make me wonder if I am wrong about her competency.

Women sympathize with each other when they make mistakes. Men think mistakes should be rectified and forgotten. You do not get a bonus in the business world for calling attention to mistakes. You are evaluated by the timing and quality of the end result. Susan only lowered Tyrone's opinion of her by talking about her mistakes. Women *do* talk about their mistakes too much. We talk about mistakes because we feel awful and we want comfort. We long for sympathy, for reassurance that the world won't end. Or we are so fearful of the consequences that we hope that by admitting to our mistakes before we are caught, we won't be punished as badly. If you accept mistakes for what they are, *mistakes*, none of this is necessary.

The only thing you have to gain by advertising your mistakes is a reputation for incompetence. Not openness, not honesty, just incompetence. Talking more about your victories than your failures will make you look, and feel, more competent. And when you look and feel more competent, you can only *be* more competent.

Have you ever wondered why successful men do not seem to make very many mistakes? The answer is very simple. Think back to the interview at the beginning of this chapter. The lawyer I quoted couldn't remember any mistakes he'd made. How many mistakes do you think he really made? How many do you think he *talked* about? How many do you think anybody ever *heard* about?

Successful men share a common attitude toward mistakes. If you make a mistake and you know how to fix it, fix it. If you make a mistake and you fix it, it is not worth mentioning. If you need help in rectifying an error, ask for help. Then fix it. If you cannot correct the error, minimize the damages. Then forget it.

## Changing Your Behavior

If fear of mistakes is one of your self-defeating behaviors, you *can* change your attitude. Begin by using your powers of observation to learn how other people handle mistakes. How do the men in your office deal with their mistakes—if they remember any? Note when and how politicians acknowledge their mistakes. Listen to what top male and female athletes say. Attend to the way very successful men and women in any field respond to their mistakes.

For instance, politicians make very visible mistakes. Their errors are publicized. They lose elections and then run for office again. Mistakes do not stop them. But a politician will only mention his mistakes when someone points them out. The politician's response may be to admit to having "misspoken" and change the subject. He may acknowledge his mistake, but then he instantly declares that he has learned something very positive from his error and talks only about these positive things. A sharp politician can phrase the way he talks about a failure as if the failure were a success.

Professional athletes impress me the most. A top athlete always responds to his mistakes by acknowledging them, analyzing them, and then correcting them. Even if you dislike sports, watch the postgame wrap-up on television. Whenever an athlete makes a major error, sportscasters invariably interview that athlete after the game. The commentators always begin the interview with something like, "You must feel like a jerk for dropping the ball." Regardless of the sport, these athletes have a similar response. It goes something like this:

> Well, this wasn't my best game. I've worked hard training and I will work even harder. Obviously I need to practice this. We're playing the Bruisers next week and I'll be out there and I'll sure be doing my best.

After watching how others respond to their mistakes, allow yourself to make some of your own. Difficult as it seems, the most effective way to get over fear of mistakes is to *make* mistakes, lots of them—and publicly. Take a wrong turn while driving with friends to a movie. Leave out an ingredient in a recipe you are cooking. I'm not suggesting you endanger anyone's life or risk lifelong embarrassment. Little mistakes are just as good as big ones.

Learn something new and difficult for you. You will make plenty of mistakes while you learn. I recommend learning a competitive team sport. But if you do not have the time, energy, or interest that a team sport requires, challenge yourself in some other way. Try things at which you know you will fail at first. Any new skill, from sewing to plastering to backgammon, will do. Improvise . . . just make mistakes!

I know that what I am advocating is easy to say and hard to do. Hard, yes; impossible, no. Here are ten suggestions that will make this difficult task easier:

1. Start in private. Before you believe you won't be drawn and quartered by others for making a mistake, you have to know that you won't punish yourself. First, try something difficult when no one else is around. Draw, paint, bake a complicated pastry. Try plumbing, plastering, woodworking, knitting, sewing. It doesn't matter how crude your handiwork; no one but you will see it.

2. Listen and realize what you say to yourself when you make a mistake. Our self-talk is so automatic that we are often unaware of it. When you make a mistake, take the time to listen to what you are telling yourself. You may find yourself thinking thoughts like these: "You jerk, you never get anything right." "What made you think you could do that?" "What a clod you are."

3. Practice being kind to yourself when you do make a mistake. If you are berating yourself for your mistake, STOP! Remind yourself that you get more flies with honey than with vinegar. If the comments you make to yourself sound like, "Almost isn't good enough, you dope!", replace them *immediately* with

something encouraging like, "Good try! I'll do it even better next time."

4. Evaluate your level of fear. Ask yourself, "What is the worst thing that can happen if I make a mistake?" Will the world end? Will anybody die? Is the level of fear you are experiencing warranted by the reality of the situation? Probably not.

5. Be prepared to make a mistake. Think up all the mistakes you could make in a given situation. Then prepare a remedy for each of these potential mistakes. Doing this will help you break the "self-punishing" habit. If you do make one of these mistakes, praise yourself for having an excellent remedy at your fingertips. If you make an unanticipated mistake, praise yourself for your creativity.

6. Confront your need to be liked. Are you really concerned about the negative consequences of your action, or are you more afraid of someone's disapproval? You are in the majority if your answer is "disapproval." Is the person you are concerned about really unlikely to forgive you? If she is, so what?

7. Purposely make a mistake in public. You make many decisions every day ranging from what shoes to wear to whom to hire for an important position. I'm sure you can find one where it will do no real damage if you are wrong. Making a mistake on purpose will give you enough distance to observe how others react to you. Are you paying more attention to your mistake than anyone else? Are you embarrassed? Remind yourself that nobody really dies of embarrassment.

8. Try risking small and unimportant mistakes. Prac-

tice your encouraging self-talk. Respond to yourself as you would respond to someone you love. Don't take on too much. Your goal is to convince yourself that mistakes don't hurt. Give yourself time to learn these new attitudes.

9. Increase the magnitude of the mistakes you risk in very small steps. If you can't sing very well, don't sing at the office party until you are completely comfortable singing in front of one person, then two, and so on. I equate this with training. Athletes don't go for the gold until they have had lots of practice.

10. Replace the habit of punishing yourself for your mistakes with rewarding yourself for your achievements. Always take the time to congratulate yourself for successes. Too many of us berate ourselves for our mistakes but just go on when we do it right without giving ourselves any praise. Rewarding and congratulating yourself is an essential step. Don't leave it out.

Making mistakes is a part of life. It is impossible to learn anything new without making some mistakes along the way. Use your sense of humor to help yourself along. Stop the negative self-talk and find something funny in your error; it's always there. If you can correct your mistake, correct it and forget it. Mistakes that are rectified are no longer mistakes. Learn what you can from your mistakes and move on. Talk to others about your successes, not your failures. Take risks. Without a fear of mistakes, you will be more comfortable embarking on new and difficult endeavors. The ability to tolerate mistakes will give you a boost up the ladder of success. Practice making mistakes. The result will be worth the effort.

## CHAPTER TWELVE

# Passivity

We have all experienced moments of passivity. Most of us are passive in some situations and not in others. Passivity is the feeling that keeps people from acting in their own best interests, from standing up for themselves, and from openly expressing their feelings. It inhibits people of both sexes, but it is far more prevalent in women than in men.

Passivity grows out of the belief that you are not important, that your ideas, opinions, and feelings don't matter or are not worth expressing. If you believe that others are better, stronger, or more important than you, it makes sense to approach the world cautiously. You try to appease others and avoid conflict. You feel safest expressing yourself in a hesitant, self-effacing manner. It becomes impossible to make decisions, be definitive, or initiate action.

In order to be assertive, you have to respect yourself as much as you respect others. We all like ourselves best when we are honest, straightforward, and decisive. Life is easier when we make things happen. It feels better to act than be acted upon. When you act assertively, you feel strong and in control. Acting passively leaves you feeling resentful and anxious. Ironically, although a passive person is trying to please others, he often creates the opposite response. The responses a passive person is most likely to create are anger, impatience, and pity. Think about how often you have felt frustrated by someone who is being too accommodating.

Common as it is, passivity is not a natural state. Activeness is a basic human need. People have an innate drive for competence. Babies are born assertive. They instinctively cry for attention when they need something. Unfortunately, active babies all too often become passive adults. What happens to children after birth to produce passivity?

## Baby-Taming Machines

We learn passivity over the years. A psychiatrist friend jokingly called families "baby-taming machines." As in all humor, this description is partly true. When families teach children good manners and consideration, they also encourage passivity. We teach children not to speak out of place and not to be disrespectful. "Do as I say." "Listen to your teachers."

Schools reward quiet, well-behaved children who don't question authority. Religions teach devotion and faithfulness to their principles. Employers want workers who can follow orders. Society could not exist if everyone did whatever they wanted, whenever they wanted. But the price we pay for a smoothly functioning society is passivity.

Our culture encourages women to assume a dependent role and present themselves as helpless. In 1992, the American Association of University Women and the National Education Association jointly published a study of teachers' responses to boys and girls in the classroom. The study was aptly named "How Schools Shortchange Girls."[1] Unfortunately, it found that schools really do encourage passivity in girls. Parents and teachers tell boys and girls to be well behaved, but they wink at boys who break the rules. We describe mischievous boys as "all boy" and very quiet girls as "little ladies." We encourage boys to be competitive and aggressive in their play while we encourage girls to be cooperative and nurturant. The words "male" and "female" connote aggression and passivity respectively.

In her article "Work Inhibitions in Women,"[2] Dr. Irene P. Stiver summarizes her analysis of work inhibitions in women. She makes the connection between women's common problems at work and our society's definition of femininity and socialization of women. From early on, we teach girls to do for others before they do for themselves. The result is that women feel selfish and opportunistic when acting on their own interests and motivations. It is fine for women to use their strength and initiative on someone else's behalf, but not on their own.

Acting assertively runs counter to the female stereotype. Some women feel that acting assertively is a threat to their female identity. If we think that passive, dependent women are feminine, what can we think about assertive women? Unfortunately, successful women do run the risk of being called unfeminine, aggressive, destructive, or castrating. We warn young girls that success may jeopardize their femininity and attractiveness to men. By the time they are teenagers, many bright girls have learned to keep their good grades to themselves.

Feeling powerful and successful threatens the female identity in other ways. A woman's identity is rooted in relationships. Some women fear that if they become too successful, they won't need anybody. If they don't need anybody, will they still feel like women? Women learn to idealize men and see them as stronger and more powerful. What do you do if you are "doing better" than the man you are trying to idealize? The prospect of being assertive and successful is colored by negative consequences like social rejection, disapproval, and the loss of femininity.

Why do so many competent women feel insecure while less competent men feel so self-assured? Studies of the different ways men and women explain their successes and failures provide the answer.[3] Feelings of self-confidence grow out of successes. Men attribute their successes to their abilities and their failures to events outside their control. Women do just the opposite. Women attribute their successes to luck and their failures to lack of ability.

This pattern is especially debilitating to bright girls. A study of preadolescents found that the brighter the boy, the better he expected to do in the future and the more he attributed his good scores to his competence.[4] Girls responded differently. The brighter the girl, the less she expected to do better in the future and the more unlikely she was to attribute her good scores to her own competence. It is impossible to feel competent if you believe your successes are due to luck and your failures are your fault.

You have to believe in yourself. If you don't believe you are competent, neither will anyone else. This lack of self-confidence hurts working women. Women end up being passive in the workplace because they feel insecure. I listen to successful women doubt their abilities and competence. I watch women reduce their effectiveness and negate their intellect and ambitions. I hear bright women expressing themselves in apologetic, diffident, self-effacing ways.

Successful women often worry about being impostors. They feel like phonies and frauds and are afraid of being found out. In my groups, for example, women ask if they are being "professional"—something men rarely worry about. When the women said "professional," I found out what they really meant was "like a man." This "professional man" they were trying to emulate was always strong, confident, self-sufficient, and unemotional at work. No wonder they felt themselves lacking. They were measuring themselves against an impossible standard.

The submissive, passive female role is just the opposite of the style needed in the competitive atmosphere of the workplace. Ironically, even though men may feel more comfortable with passive women in social situations, they feel frustrated when female coworkers exhibit this trait. The complaints men voiced most often about passivity were: women apologize too much and women are too tentative.

## Apologizing

Luther, a chemist, grumbled:

> Women apologize all the time. I wish they would just do their work.

Do you apologize too much? Do you apologize every time you do something that makes someone else unhappy? Do you apologize when someone expresses displeasure even if it is not your fault? As a test, count the number of times a day you say you are sorry. Or better yet, log all the times and reasons you say you are sorry for a week. Until we focus on it, most of us are unaware of how often we apologize.

Apologizing is a deeply ingrained habit. Women say "I'm sorry" for a myriad of reasons. We say we are sorry to smooth troubled waters or to stop someone from being angry with us. We say we are sorry to express sympathy or regret. We apologize when we ask for someone's attention. We apologize when we correct someone.

"I'm sorry to bother you."
"I'm sorry you lost that contract."
"I'm sorry but you're wrong."
"I'm sorry you're feeling badly."

The only appropriate time to apologize is when you feel sorry for something you *did*. Expressing sympathy by saying "I'm sorry" is confusing to men. Have you ever said, "I'm sorry you had a bad day," to a man you like, only to have him bark at you and say, "Why? It wasn't your fault."

Women are expert at sensing when someone is unhappy and soothing upset feelings. But in business, men do not want to be soothed. They just want the problem fixed. You may be trying to be helpful by saying something like "I'm sorry we lost that account," but men find such comments an annoying distraction, or worse yet, an insult. Remember Rule 2: Act strong. If you acknowledge that a man is upset, he may feel you are pointing out his weakness. If you cannot fix the problem, don't try to be comforting. Your attempts are likely to backfire.

It takes practice to learn to allow someone to remain angry or upset. Many women feel uncomfortable around someone who is upset. You have to become comfortable with the feeling you get when someone is displeased with you—or when someone is displeased with anything at all. It is not your responsibility to make everyone feel good. What you are paid to do is to do your job well.

When someone is angry, stop and think. Is it your fault? If it isn't, bite your tongue if you have to, but don't apologize. Is it something you can fix? If it is, don't apologize, just fix it. Is it something you've already remedied? Then why apologize if the problem has been solved? I am not saying never apologize, just be sure your apologies are really warranted.

## Too Tentative

Carlos, a doctor, described a woman he did not hire:

> She was so tentative I was afraid to be alone in the same
> room with her. I was worried that if there were a fire,
> she wouldn't tell me because she wouldn't want to in-
> terrupt me.

Tentative. Hesitant. Diffident. Timid. Uncertain. Unsure. These
were the words men used most often when describing women
they considered incompetent. Even if you are sure of yourself,
you sound tentative if you hesitate in your answers, speak in a
meek voice, or use too many qualifying words like "probably,"
"almost," "many," "some," "usually" in your speech. To avoid
sounding tentative, speak loudly with certainty, don't hesitate,
and use a minimum of qualifiers.

Do you use too many qualifiers? There are times when qualifying words are essential, but how often do you say "some," "almost," "most," or "somewhat"? Are you using these words to be
precise or because you are reluctant to be definitive? Count how
often you use qualifying words—then work at leaving all qualifiers out of your vocabulary. You will not *always* be *exactly* correct, but you will sound definitive.

As an experiment, one of my problem-solving groups
agreed to talk in sentences no longer than five words. We had
to stick to the bare facts and eliminate qualifying words. We
all laughed because we sounded like a group of men. Try this
yourself. You will be surprised at how many of the qualifying
words are unnecessary and how definitive you sound when you
leave them out.

Some women have breathy, soft voices. Men interpret these
as weak and don't take these women seriously. I asked a voice

coach what these women could do to sound strong. She told me that sounding strong is also a problem for men. The problem is not volume but lack of projection. Her solution is to teach her clients to project their voices. This simple change makes a big difference. An excellent way to learn to project is to learn to sing. Take a class, join a chorus, or just sing in the shower. The result will be gratifying.

Assertive behavior is not just what you say. It is a combination of what you say, how you say it, and how you look while you are saying it. We communicate our strength with words, body language, and facial expressions.

Be aware of how you look as well as the words you use. The way you express yourself is as important as what you say. Make eye contact. Look directly at the person to whom you are speaking. Be sure that your facial expression agrees with the message you want to convey. Don't express anger while smiling or laughing. Face the person you are speaking to. Hold your head erect. Speak slowly and clearly and use a well-modulated conversational tone.

## Is Passivity Hampering You?

Ask yourself these questions:

1. Are you comfortable taking risks?
2. Will you volunteer for a difficult assignment that you have never done before?
3. Are you afraid to ask for more interesting work because you might not know how to do it?
4. Do you have difficulty making decisions?
5. Does it take you longer to do your work than the men around you?

6. Do you fill your reports with every conceivable detail, afraid you will leave something out?
7. Are you more likely to ask a supervisor to make a major decision rather than make it for yourself?
8. Do you apologize for things you didn't do?
9. When someone is unfair, do you call it to his attention?
10. Can you say no to unreasonable requests?
11. Do you return merchandise you don't want?
12. Do you send back food that is improperly prepared?
13. Can you say no to a salesperson who has spent time trying to please you?
14. Do you speak out when someone cuts ahead of you in line?
15. Are you comfortable saying no when a friend asks for a favor?
16. Do you speak up in meetings?
17. Will you give in on a point because your opponent sounds more confident?
18. Are you waiting for a mentor to approach you?
19. Do you think no one would want to mentor you?
20. Is the worry that you will be a bother or pest keeping you from asking someone to be your mentor?

If you answered no to questions 1, 2, or 9 through 16, or yes to questions 3 to 8 or 17 through 20, you have uncovered an area where passivity is getting in your way.

## Changing Your Behavior

Assertive behavior is a skill you can learn. But in order to act assertively, you have to believe you are worthwhile. You have to believe you should be treated with respect. You have to value and respect yourself.

You have the right to expect people to listen to you and take you seriously. You have the right to say no without feeling guilty. You have the right to ask for what you want. You even have the right to choose not to assert yourself.

You don't have to step on people to be assertive. Everyone has the right to express their thoughts and feelings. If you ask for what you want, the other person doesn't have to give it to you. He also has the right to say no. Everyone has the same rights. Treat others the way you want others to treat you. Just be sure you treat yourself as well as you treat others. Respect other people's rights, but don't forget to respect your own.

Some women are reluctant to act assertively because they are afraid of hurting someone. However, never hurting anyone in any circumstance is an impossible goal. Sometimes the only way not to hurt someone else is to hurt yourself. Do you deserve to be hurt all the time? If we treat ourselves without respect, we teach others to treat us the same way. If you don't take care of yourself, you won't be able to help anyone else.

When you hold back your criticism because you don't want to hurt someone's feelings, you are insulting that person. You are assuming he is incapable of speaking up for himself or that he is not strong enough to take any criticism. If you don't tell someone you don't like his behavior, you don't give that person a chance to change. Not sharing ourselves with others by not telling them how we think and feel is every bit as selfish as not caring about their feelings.

Some women won't act assertively because they don't want anyone to get angry with them. This is another impossible goal. People get angry with us when we don't give them what they want. But what if what they want is not good for them or very hurtful for you? If you are right, you are being irresponsible if you don't hold your ground when someone is arguing with you. It is unpleasant when someone you respect is angry with you, but sometimes disagreeing with them is the kindest thing you can do.

You don't have to be assertive all the time, but you should be free to act assertively anytime you choose. You should not be inhibited from acting a certain way. When you are unsure whether or not to act assertively in a given situation, ask yourself these questions:

- What exactly is my goal?
- How important is this situation to me?
- How do I usually handle this situation?
- How will acting assertively help me achieve my goal?
- Do I have anything to lose by acting assertively?
- How will I feel if I don't assert myself?
- What is stopping me from being assertive?

These questions will help you clarify your thinking. They will help you weigh what you would gain by being assertive against any possible losses. If you decide you would like to act assertively in the situation but are having difficulty, the next step is to examine the reasons why you have not been acting assertively.

To uncover what is holding you back, ask yourself:

- What exactly is it I want to do?
- What do I think will happen if I do it?
- How does that make me feel?

Psychology owes a big debt to Dr. Aaron Beck for developing Cognitive Therapy,[5] a special way of understanding the way we think and feel. Dr. Beck teaches us that our emotions are not a response to a particular situation, but a response to the way we think about a situation. We react to what we *believe* about a situation, what we *believe* our responsibilities and resources are, and how we *think* others will respond. The core of Cognitive Therapy is that underneath our negative emotions is an underlying assumption about the situation that is faulty. To understand our feelings, we have to examine *more* than just the situation. We have to look at how we are evaluating that situation.

Underlying our emotions are assumptions we take for granted. By evaluating and correcting these assumptions, we can change our feelings and our behaviors. Sometimes the beliefs are general, like "Don't inconvenience anybody" or "Don't make anyone mad." Other times they are beliefs specific to a situation, like "He will be furious if I give him more work." Or "If I ask for clarification, he'll think I am the stupidest person in the world."

Don't follow your assumptions blindly. Challenge your beliefs. Take a piece of paper and fold it in half. On one side of the page write what you are thinking about a situation. Use the other side to argue with yourself, to question the responses you anticipate. Doing this in writing is important. It gives you some distance. As an example, I'll illustrate how to rebut the assumptions from the previous paragraph.

| | |
|---|---|
| "Don't inconvenience anybody." | Does "don't inconvenience anybody" mean it's always at my expense? Why should I always be the one to be inconvenienced? I am somebody, too. |
| "Don't make anyone mad." | I can't control other people's emotions. Some people get |

| | angry for no good reason. If he gets mad, he will get over it. |
|---|---|
| "He will be furious if I give him more work." | He may surprise me and be more rational than I think. If he isn't, will the world end if he gets mad? |
| "If I ask for clarification, he'll think I am the stupidest person in the world." | He may think I am wise to ask. He would rather I ask questions than make mistakes. What if he does think I'm stupid? Well, he won't think I am very smart if I don't ask for clarification and do the whole thing wrong. |

Whenever you are frightened to be assertive, examine your feelings and question your assumptions. Fear is a rational response to danger, but are you facing any *real* danger? Before you say yes, examine the situation. You will be surprised how often your fear does not seem rational once you clarify it for yourself.

The most common reason people are reluctant to be assertive is fear that someone will get angry. When you are concerned about someone's anger, ask yourself what will happen if he is angry. Most of the time the answer is nothing terrible. "If I get this wrong, will he kill me?" How many employees has he killed in the last year? You may feel pained if someone is angry at you, but your demise is unlikely.

Both thoughts and behavior are important in personal growth. If you change one, the other will follow. It doesn't matter which comes first. Question your beliefs. Ask yourself, "What is the evidence that proves my assumption? What is the *worst* thing that can happen?" And then see if the "worst" thing is really so bad.

Be assertive with yourself. Convince yourself to take the needed actions. Don't be deterred by less than perfect results. Start with small steps and expect failures. Keep going after setbacks.

Once you have decided to be assertive, how do you do it? Start by imagining yourself acting assertively in the situation. If you are not sure how, watch or ask someone you respect. Plan what you will say ahead of time. Rehearse. Role-play with a friend. Start with similar but easy situations and increase the difficulty as you succeed. Work up to the hard ones.

Don't accept passivity in yourself. You will like yourself better if you are assertive. You are more effective when you are assertive. Remember that assertion is a skill you can learn. Take advantage of the many excellent assertiveness training books or courses that are available.

I've summarized the steps to learning assertive behaviors in the "Ten Steps to Change," which follow. Use them to modify your behavior. Be patient with yourself and don't skip any steps. The time and energy you invest learning assertion will be worth it.

# TEN STEPS TO CHANGE

**STEP ONE: OBSERVE AND RECORD YOUR BEHAVIOR.**

1. How many opportunities did you have to be assertive?

2. How often did you ask for what you want?

3. How often did you say what you really meant?

4. How often did you wish you were more assertive?

**STEP TWO: LOOK FOR A PATTERN.**

1. In what situations are you most assertive?

2. In what situations are you most passive?

3. With whom are you most assertive?

4. With whom are you most passive?

5. Create a list of situations in which you would like to be more assertive. Rank them from easiest to hardest.

**STEP THREE: CHOOSE AN EFFECTIVE MODEL—AN ASSERTIVE PERSON.**

1. What do you like about her style?

2. How is her behavior different from yours?

3. What makes her so effective?

4. Ask her how she would think and feel in situations that make you uncomfortable.

5. If you don't want to emulate a real person, study a TV, movie, or book character.

## STEP FOUR: CHOOSE A SITUATION IN WHICH YOU WOULD HAVE LIKED TO BE MORE ASSERTIVE.

1. Record the way you responded in that situation.

   a. How did you behave?

   b. How did you feel?

   c. What were you thinking?

   d. What was the result?

2. How could you have handled it better?

## STEP FIVE: IMAGINE YOURSELF HANDLING THE SITUATION EFFECTIVELY IN A STYLE THAT IS COMFORTABLE FOR YOU.

1. Visualize the situation in detail.

   a. What are you thinking?

   b. How do you feel?

   c. What will you say?

2. Picture the result.

3. How will you feel when you achieve your goal?

4. Picture alternative responses to that situation. (There is always more than one way to effectively handle every situation.)

   a. How are they different?

   b. What are the benefits and drawbacks of each?

   c. Imagine yourself trying out different responses.

STEP SIX: TRY HANDLING A SITUATION LIKE THE ONE YOU IMAGINED.

1. Start with an easy situation.

2. Choose a supportive environment.

STEP SEVEN: EVALUATE THE RESULTS.

1. Get feedback, if possible.

2. If you are pleased with the result:

    a. Note what worked.

    b. Pay attention to how good you feel.

    c. Reward yourself.

3. If you did not get the result you wanted:

    a. What was the result?

    b. How did the other person respond?

    c. What went wrong?

    d. What response would have produced a better result?

    e. Ask for help if you are stumped.

    f. Vividly imagine yourself responding differently.

    g. TRY AGAIN!

STEP EIGHT: TRY YOUR NEW RESPONSES IN INCREASINGLY DIFFICULT SITUATIONS.

1. Go from easiest to hardest to assure more successes than failures.

2. Move on to your next-hardest situation when you have become successful at the easier one.

3. Don't get discouraged when you don't succeed. Nobody succeeds all the time.

4. It isn't always easy. Give yourself a push if you need it and keep trying.

STEP NINE: EVALUATE THE RESULTS EACH TIME AS IN STEP SEVEN.

1. Keep a log of your attempts at assertion and your results.

2. Take the time to evaluate each of these situations.

   a. What worked well?

   b. What doesn't work?

   c. What are you thinking?

   d. How do you feel?

STEP TEN: KEEP AT IT.

1. Take baby steps. Don't be impatient and try to do too much too soon.

2. ALWAYS reward yourself for your successes.

3. If you fail, congratulate yourself for trying and then try again.

4. Continue to record your behavior and watch your assertiveness skills grow.

## CHAPTER THIRTEEN

# Difficulty Prioritizing

We all have too much to do. There is too little time to do our work and too little time to keep our personal lives in order. The basics of everyday life, like cleaning, shopping, cooking, and doing the laundry are time-consuming. If you are trying to maintain a relationship or raising children, the demands on you are even greater. There are just so many hours in the day. If you can't work any harder at your job because of lack of time, you have to work smarter. And working smarter means prioritizing.

I asked the most efficient businesswomen I interviewed to share their secrets. Every one of them stressed the importance of keeping lists. They all used some kind of to-do list. The formats of the list varied from commercial organizers to computer programs to a piece of plain paper. You should find the most comfortable method for you.

Cecilia, VP of human resources in a swiftly growing company, looked at my desk and shook her head. "I don't know how you work like that. I keep only one piece of paper on my desk at a time." She stopped me as I began to defend my various piles of paper. "Why have them all out on your desk? They are distracting. You can only work on one of them at any given moment." She's right.

Lucy is the only woman at her level in a very male organization. I asked her how she did it. "I'm very efficient. I try to touch every piece of paper only once."

Tippy, VP of sales, said, "You can waste 50 percent of your time going through papers on your desk. Each time you sit down, you look through everything. And when you come back from lunch, you do it all over again."

These women are masters at prioritizing. Not being a master myself, I tried their suggestions. I feel as if I added an extra hour to my day. You can do the same. In this chapter, I will discuss the most common problems that interfere with efficiency and offer some suggestions to solve them.

## Failing to Develop Specific, Objective Goals

KURT:
   Why do women make everything so complicated?

SUZAN:
   Men see everything as black and white!

Men and women approach problem solving so differently that it sometimes seems as if they are trying to solve different problems. This is not an illusion. They frame the problems so differently that they become different problems. Men define a problem by the facts of the case. To a woman, a problem includes more than just the facts. It includes the people, their relationships to each other, and how the solution will affect everyone involved. I think the broader female mode of thinking increases the opportunity for creativity. Adding concerns about the impact of decisions on people and relationships enriches business decision making. But seeing so many aspects of a situation can also obscure the essential points and make finding the solution more difficult.

The key to getting the best of both worlds is to define the problem you are trying to solve or the result you are trying to achieve concretely and specifically. When you know exactly what you are trying to accomplish, you can weigh every fact, argument, and offer against this goal.

The way you define a problem determines your route to the solution. If your goal is clear, you can weigh the way each fact affects your goal. This simplifies and clarifies the work you have to do. You may be surprised at how much information you include that does not directly affect your goal, and your argument will be more powerful if you leave this extra information out.

In a negotiation, for example, you should be able to summarize your position on one page. Then you have what is really important right in front of you. You will look organized to your opponent and your outline will keep you to the point. If your opponent distracts you, you have your summary to refocus you.

When I am having difficulty making a decision or solving a problem, I go through these steps to clarify my thinking. I learned this technique from two creative psychologists, Dr. Marvin Goldfried and Dr. Thomas D'Zurilla.[1] Try it the next time you are having trouble solving a confusing problem or are deadlocked in a negotiation. It is very effective for problem solving and decision making.

1. Define the problem clearly and concretely.
   a. What do you want to change?
   b. What result do you want to achieve?
2. Think up as many different solutions to this problem as you can. Allow your imagination free rein. Think up some "unrealistic" solutions as well as some traditional ones.
3. What would the result of each of these solutions be? Allowing yourself to consider some unrealistic or

unorthodox solutions can give you the creative jolt
you need.

4. Evaluate the results of each of your solutions and
choose the one that you think will get you the best
result.

5. Try it out. If you get the result you wanted or a result
you are satisfied with, congratulations. If not . . .

6. Evaluate what went wrong and try again, using the
new information you learned on your last attempt.

## Overpreparation

Are you working harder than you have to? Are you putting more
time and effort into a task than it deserves? These are hard questions to answer. If it takes you longer to do the same work as
your male colleagues, or if your reports are longer than everyone
else's, you probably overprepare. Both the men and the women I
interviewed agreed that women often put more time and energy
into a task than is necessary to get the job done.

Is your work too detailed? Doing too good a job is a strange
criticism, but it is a criticism often leveled against women. One
of women's strengths is attention to detail, but it is also one of
their weaknesses. Men complain of having to spend too much
time reading unnecessarily detailed reports. The extra details
made the reports confusing.

Two common reasons for including too many details are insecurity and not feeling you know your material well enough.
There is a sailor's saying, "If you can't tie good knots, tie lots of
them." We could say the same thing about facts. If you are not
sure you have a good argument, make lots of them. But when a
sailor sees a bundle of knots, he knows they were tied by an un-

skilled person. When you hear too many facts, you know the presenter does not really know what he is talking about. When you include too many details, you sound unfocused rather than expert. If you can't decide which facts are important and which are not, you may have to learn more about your material.

But I think insecurity presents a bigger problem for women than not knowing their material. We overprepare because we are insecure. It takes self-confidence to decide how much work is enough. We include every detail for fear of leaving something out. It is easier to include every fact about an issue than to choose which points are necessary to advance your case.

Many women are hampered by perfectionism. They want to do a perfect job every time. Not only is it unnecessary to be perfect all the time, it is unproductive. Are you thinking "I always want to do the best job I can. What's wrong with striving for perfection?" The answer is in how you define "best job." Pragmatically, the best job is the one that achieves the needed result with the least amount of time and energy.

Different assignments require different amounts of attention to detail. There are times when it is better to do a mediocre job than not do it at all. Often, what you consider mediocre is more than adequate for the purpose. It is a waste of time and energy to write a very detailed and accurate report when your supervisor would have been happier with a quick and dirty solution. The extra time you spent making that report perfect will be resented, not appreciated.

You can avoid overpreparation if you are very clear about your goals and if you respect your skills. Before you start an assignment, ask yourself:

- What result are you trying to accomplish?
- What will the information you are researching be used for?

- Who will it be presented to?
- How will it be presented?

*Trust your skills and your instincts.* Work hard enough to get the job done, but no more. If you have the time and energy to do a perfect job, by all means do so. But if your time is limited, remember, perfection is not your goal. Winning is.

## Problems Delegating

Do you have trouble delegating? Many women do. Here are some typical comments:

> I'd rather do it myself than go to all the trouble of telling someone else how to do it.
> If I do it, I know it will be done right.
> If I delegate and it isn't done correctly, I'm responsible.

The ability to delegate work is an essential skill. Skillful delegating takes time and assertiveness. It increases your productivity, but it does have some drawbacks. When you delegate, you give up some control over the work and you may have to accept work that is adequate but not as good as yours would have been.

But you lose much more by not delegating. If you don't delegate, it takes longer to finish projects. You risk becoming mired in routine work and not having time for new, challenging assignments. You won't have time to learn new skills or be creative. If you don't have time to volunteer for assignments to display your skills, you hurt your chances of advancement. In most companies, ability to delegate is one of the criteria used to evaluate managers.

Delegating multiplies your productivity. Delegating some of your work frees you up to use your time more effectively. You can take on more important projects. When you have the time to be creative, you can develop more effective techniques to do your work. You can make your department more productive.

Delegating is also cost-effective for your organization. An hour of your time is more expensive than an hour of your subordinate's. When you delegate part of your work, not only do you get more work done cheaply, you also give your subordinates a chance to grow. Your subordinates will appreciate this and feel more challenged, motivated, and involved. By delegating, you build up their loyalty and respect.

If you are unsure if you should delegate a task, ask yourself these questions:

- Will it be cost-effective for me to do the task myself?
- Can someone else do it as well as or better than I can?
- Do I have the time to do it well myself or am I likely to do it poorly because of lack of time?
- Can a subordinate do the job well enough for the cost or time involved?
- If a subordinate can't do it as well as I can, but I have something more important to do:
  — Can I coach anyone adequately on how to do it?
  — Can I keep adequate control over the project?
  — Am I willing to accept less than perfect results?

Successful delegation requires understanding the skills, needs, attitudes, and preferences of each subordinate. Always try to find a fit between the task, the person, and the situation. Delegating requires comfort with assertion and tact. Nobody responds well to "Do this!" Your sensitivity and responsiveness to others are a real advantage here.

To get the best results when you delegate, explain your goals and objectives in concrete measurable details.

- What must be done.
- Why it is being done.
- How well it must be done.
- When it must be completed.

Be sure your employee has the skill, authority, and access to the necessary resources to do the job effectively. Try to plan some training as part of the process. When you describe the task, also explain how you plan to evaluate the results. Always take the time to thank your employee and acknowledge the work that went into the task.

You may find delegating difficult and time-consuming at first. Keep at it; it gets easier. In the long run, the time savings and increase in productivity make it worth the effort.

## DO'S AND DON'TS OF GOOD DELEGATION

Do:

- Feel secure and confident in your role as manager.
- Have confidence in your subordinate's abilities.
- Be clear and direct when explaining the assignment.
- Allow your employees to use their own methods and creativity whenever possible.

- Be willing to accept delegated work that is less than perfect.
- Criticize fairly, objectively, and constructively.
- Acknowledge and reward good performance.

DON'T:

- Delay asking subordinates to do work for fear they will feel overburdened.
- Become paralyzed by fear of criticism and end up doing all the work yourself.
- Be afraid of being shown up by your subordinates.
- Be insensitive to your employee's feelings.
- Hover over your employees after delegating, giving directions and making them feel like children.
- Snatch back the task in midstream without explanation.
- Criticize employees in front of others.

## Failing to Define Long-Term Career Goals

Many women in the workplace today would echo this comment from Anna, a businesswoman in her forties.

Career goals! How could I have set career goals when I never thought I would have a career in the first place?

Ernest, owner of an automobile dealership, agrees:

> It's easier for men than for women. Lots of women
> thought they would just work for a while. I always knew
> I would have to earn a living.

Traditionally, men have careers; women have jobs. If you think
you have a job rather than a career, take the time to reevaluate.
Try to think of the job you have now as one step in your long-
range career plan.

Careers have to be planned over the long run. Tim, a mortgage banker, likened planning to the backhand in tennis: the
way you bring the racket back determines the quality of your
stroke. Even if you are well into your career, you can still plan
the rest of it.

When you join a company, know what you want from that
association. Your long-range goals don't have to be conventional.
You can include taking time out, or working part-time when you
raise your children, as part of your path. Your career path will be
different from that of someone who doesn't take time off—not
better or worse, just different.

You can always reevaluate and change your plan. Life is un-
predictable. In the course of your life, you may change your career plan several times. But you always need a long-term plan. If
you don't set clear goals for yourself, you never get the pleasure
of realizing that you've met them.

## Appearing Unfocused

Frequently, very efficient women look inefficient to men. Men
commonly complain, "Women are all over the place. They take

forever to get to the point." Women are not all over the place. Women reach conclusions. But they take a very different route from men to get there.

Men and women think differently. Men think linearly. They like to go in a straight line from question to answer. A leads to B leads to C. Women think globally. Rather than isolate a few facts and only focus on them, women consider the whole field at once. They see many facets to a given problem and try to include all these facets in their thinking. Men limit the number of facets they consider in order to follow a straight road from question to answer. For women, the people and their relationships to each other are part of a problem. Men stick to the facts and consider the people and their relationships to be extraneous.

When discussing a problem, women include the details they find important. Most of these details, especially the ones about people, seem irrelevant to men. Men complain that women are "all over the place" or "never get to the point" because they don't understand why women are mentioning so many details that seem irrelevant to them.

If you want your work to be understood by a man, you have to present it in a language he can understand. Your presentation is as important as the facts themselves. Men will stop listening if they think you are bringing in too many "irrelevant" details. You don't have to change your way of thinking to solve this male-female communication problem, you just have to change your presentation.

To sound convincing and authoritative to a man, introduce each point clearly and deliberately, explain the point, and then summarize it. Men want the minimum amount of information necessary to make a decision. Start by giving just the major points. Show how each point is essential and directly relevant to your conclusion. Don't worry about giving too little information. If he wants to know more, he will ask.

Sarah Jane, a successful corporate trainer, passed on this helpful tip:

> Instead of stating your case as you normally would, number your points and announce the number before each point. Don't change anything about your presentation, just add the number. "Point one is X, point two is Y, point three is Z." Whenever I do this, the men compliment me on my clear, logical thinking. Try it. It works every time.

# PART FOUR

# TACTICS MEN USE AGAINST WOMEN AND HOW TO COUNTER THOSE TACTICS

# Introduction

Nancy's experience with Art is all too common:

> I was excited about my new sales position at a major investment company. Art, my new coworker, seemed friendly and helpful. I was surprised when Fred, an old friend who is now my client, called me at home. He wanted to know why I had not returned his phone calls. Fred told me he left several messages with Art. I began to investigate. I learned that not only was Art not giving me phone messages, but he was also keeping all the leads that came into the office for himself. I also discovered that Art scheduled a meeting for me with a client, but didn't tell me about it. Art scheduled the appointment at a time he knew I would be out of town. He planned to show up himself and steal the account.

Hard work and skill are not enough to ensure success. Strategy plays an essential part. Most men are not as underhanded as Art, but they do use strategic maneuvers to beat their opponents. In many organizations, advancement is a zero-sum game. In order for someone to win, someone has to lose. The only way to advance in these organizations is to overpower or eliminate your opponents. This is an unfamiliar and disturbing concept to most women. You don't have to play dirty tricks to win in business, but you do have to know how to defend yourself against them.

Men grow up competing. They are accustomed to thinking about beating their opponents. Women don't have this reservoir of experience to draw from. Women grow up learning to be supportive and cooperative, not trying to make somebody else lose. Many women are easy targets because they don't recognize an attack until it is too late. When they do recognize an attack, they are uncomfortable about fighting back or unsure how to defend themselves.

Men use aggressive tactics against other men as well as against women. Some tactics like yelling, or storming out of a room, work well against both sexes but are especially effective against women. Other tactics, like calling a woman by her first name rather than her appropriate title, like Dr. or Ms., or playing on a woman's dislike of conflict, are targeted at women.

Unfortunately, men don't reserve these tactics for business adversaries only. They also use them on female colleagues. The women in my groups told countless stories about male colleagues using the same tactics they use against their female opponents against their female coworkers. "I thought we were all on the same team" and "They wouldn't treat a man that way," were frequent complaints I heard.

Why do some men treat female colleagues as if they were competitors? To some men, all women are their competition. For these men, everyone is on two teams at the same time. The interests of these two teams sometimes conflict. Your company and your competitor's company make up one set of teams. The other set of teams is the Boys' Team and the Girls' Team. And the Boys' Team is on the attack.

Why would men put so much energy into this secondary battle? It seems such a waste of time and energy. Margaret Mead explains it in her famous work *Male and Female*:

... maleness in America (and I would suggest, elsewhere) is not absolutely defined, it has to be kept and re-earned every day, and one essential element in the definition is beating in every game that both sexes play, in every activity in which both sexes engage.[1]

This male-female conflict is a result of the way boys develop their identities. Boys develop their masculine identity by engaging in pursuits society defines as masculine. They need places and activities clearly designated as masculine. Traditionally, they exclude girls from these places and activities. As children, boys lock girls out of their clubhouses. As they get older the boys carry this tradition to the locker room and, in adulthood, to the workplace.

In adulthood, work becomes the primary arena where men validate their self-esteem and identity. When women enter the workplace, they threaten this source of male identity. If work, or war, or sports are no longer male proving grounds because they include women, how can men prove they are masculine?

Women will face hostility when they enter these male enclaves as long as men perceive their presence as a threat to male identity. Eventually, men will adapt to the changes in our society and develop new ways to define their masculinity. But most haven't done this successfully yet. Understanding the motivation behind male hostility helps you feel less angry. Try not to take these attacks personally. It is not you he is attacking; it is any female who is invading his domain and threatening his identity. You will find it easier to defend yourself if you remain calm and clearheaded.

As a psychologist, I am sympathetic to the struggle men are facing. But sympathetic as I am, I don't think you should tolerate unwarranted hostility and abuse. You have to stop the assaults. The men I interviewed described tactics they use against women.

I am going to reveal these tactics to you and suggest ways to defend yourself against them.

I strongly urge you to join with other businesswomen to identify the tactics men are using against you. Sharing the burden lightens the load and eases some of the pain. The women in my group came up with wonderfully inventive strategies to help each other. They found it easier to be creative when they were not the one being attacked. The most effective strategies for you are ones that complement your personality. There is more than one way to counter any attack. Brainstorming with a group of women will help you develop strategies that are comfortable and effective for you.

## CHAPTER FOURTEEN

# Feminizing

The tactics I describe in this chapter derive their power from our culture's traditional stereotype of women as passive and compliant. Men use these tactics to make you look and feel like "a good little girl" rather than the competent professional you are.

Hugh, a labor negotiator, explains:

> The first thing I do when I have a female opponent is flirt. I look at her clothes, and the way she carries herself, and gauge her reaction. I want to see if I should treat her as a woman or a person.

Hugh went on to describe the different tactics he uses against women and against "people." He is very proud of his skill. Although most of the men I interviewed were not as blunt as Hugh, they all used the tactics I will describe in this chapter. There is no clear dividing line between this group of tactics and sexual harassment. It is a matter of degree. When these tactics become obnoxious enough or when enough of them are used consistently, they become sexual harassment.

## Diminutive Names

Cynthia, VP of sales:

> Bill, Jerry, Herbert, and I gave a presentation at Great
> Big Corporation. We introduced ourselves as Bill Smith,
> Jerry Jones, Herbert White, and Cynthia Hunter. The
> CEO at Great Big said, "It is a pleasure to meet you,
> gentlemen. It's also a pleasure to meet you, dear."

Has anyone addressed you as "honey," "dear," "sweetie," or some cute childish version of your name in a business meeting? Has anyone introduced you by your first name while presenting everyone else as Mr. So-and-So? When a man uses these diminutive addresses, he is trying to treat you as a woman, not a person. He is attempting to keep you in your place, to establish that your rank is lower than his. He is clearly announcing that he doesn't respect you.

If you are not sure if a man is doing this on purpose, politely ask him to address you by your last name or your title. This will clarify his motive. If he is calling you "dear" out of habit, not to insult you, he will stop or at least try to stop. If he responds rudely or makes no effort to accede to your wishes, you know that you have an enemy on your hands. Get ready to deal with him.

One way to counteract this tactic is to ignore it no matter how much it annoys you. If you don't let him know that it bothers you to be called "cutie," the tactic will not be having the desired effect and the man may stop. When a man using this as a weapon discovers that he can irritate you by calling you "hon" or "toots," you can be sure that he will continue to do it. You have shown him an effective weapon to use against you.

But there will be times when calling you a diminutive name in front of an audience affects the way the audience perceives you. When you are the only person addressed by her first name, people assume you are an assistant, not a peer. When a man consistently uses a diminutive, others begin to see that man as the father or the expert and you as the child or the novice. Unfortunately, if you look angry when you ask him to stop, you can look like a petulant child. You appear as vulnerable as he is trying to make you look.

Use your sense of humor to turn this situation around. Try to communicate amusement with your tone of voice and your posture. Looking mildly, condescendingly amused is an effective way to regain control. When you look amused rather than angry, he starts to look childish.

Jennifer, a mortgage banker, found a different approach:

> In a recent negotiation, my opponent, an older, very distinguished man, kept calling me "dear" in a conde-scending tone of voice. I knew I had to stop him. I non-chalantly began calling him "honey" when I addressed him. Evidently no one had done that before. He was taken aback and began using my name.

Jennifer's tactic was particularly effective because she was able to look as natural as he did when she used a diminutive.

When someone is calling you "babe," ask yourself how much harm it is doing. If it doesn't affect the way you feel or the way others view you, it isn't affecting your work. It may be annoying, but it is not harmful. If it makes you angry, control your feelings by reminding yourself that he is using this tactic because he can't win with just his skill. He's looking for a way to distract you. Feel sorry for the poor darlin'; he's in over his head. If you just leave him alone, he will sink.

# Chivalry

Charlotte, management consultant:

> When he held the door, pulled out my chair, and helped
> me off with my coat, I just smiled. But when he tried to
> carry my briefcase, I stopped him. He said, "I'm only being
> polite." But it wasn't his words or his actions. It was his at-
> titude. He was trying to make me look weak and helpless.

For some men, chivalry is no more than a habit. They believe
that a woman will be insulted if he doesn't act like a gentleman.
If a man like this opens doors or holds your chair, just accept it.
Most likely he is trying to show respect, not demean you.

Other men use chivalry as a weapon, to make you seem more
like a "girl" than a professional. When men use chivalry in this
way, they usually couple it with a condescending voice, exagger-
ated manners, and comments about needing to protect you.

By just being gallant, a man can make you look helpless. He
wants to send the message, "She needs my protection and I am
strong enough to protect her." But if you bristle when someone
holds your door or pulls out your chair, you appear ungracious.
You open yourself up to the criticism that you are overreacting.
When you draw attention to his behavior, you help him advertise
his message.

I think the best response is no response. If a man is using ex-
aggerated manners to needle or unnerve you and you don't respond, he will stop. However, if you think his behavior is
affecting the way other people perceive you, you may have to respond. You might say, "Thank you—no one does that anymore."
You sound appreciative while making the man look like an
anachronism. As with dealing with most of these tactics, your
sense of humor is invaluable. You can turn his chivalry to your

advantage if you can respond humorously in a way that insinuates reverence is your due and he is but a servant.

## Stereotyping

Celeste, an auditor:

> I was angry when I saw that one of my partners, Will, had changed my report. He hadn't consulted me and some of his changes were wrong. I pointed out his mistakes calmly and asked him to consult me before he made any changes in the future. I was pleased with the assertive way I handled the problem. Then I overheard him say to Joe, "Stay away from her today. She must have PMS."

Stereotypes exist.

> Blondes are stupid.
> Redheads have hot tempers.
> Women are angry because they have PMS.
> Women are too emotional.

Stereotypes are a kind of shorthand. Thinking in stereotypes is a lazy way to perceive the world. If you see everyone as a stereotype, you don't have to bother finding out who they really are.

It is difficult to get past stereotypes. Sometimes it is impossible. You may not be able to make a person who relies on stereotypes treat you as the person you are, rather than the stereotype he thinks you are. Don't feel insulted when a man puts you into a simplistic category. It's a sign of his lack of perception—not a failing of yours.

When you can't eliminate stereotyping, you can use it to your advantage. If someone is treating you as a stereotype, it means he has not sized you up properly. He doesn't know who you really are. This gives you the advantage of surprise.

If a man sees you as a passive girl and you're not one, you will catch him off guard by your competence and assertion. He will expect to win any contest with you without trying. He will not plan any defense against you because he doesn't think you will challenge him. You can just walk off with your prize.

A word of warning. When you don't respond in the passive way that he expects, be prepared for a hostile response. Your opponent will be angry that you didn't behave the way he expected you to. He will feel tricked. It doesn't matter that he was tricked by himself not by you. A man like this will back himself into a corner because he thought you were such a pushover. Then he will feel too humiliated to back down. He will be compelled to stand his ground even if the result will be disastrous for both of you.

Try to keep this type of man from boxing himself in or making a fool of himself, especially if he is a colleague you often work with. Try to anticipate this bully's behavior and help him avoid a confrontation, particularly a public one. Remember the rule about letting him save face. Use your creativity to give him an out, even if it is a weak one. Suggest you talk in private. Agree with some part of his demand. In Chapter Seventeen, "Scare Tactics," I give you more detailed advice about how to handle this kind of verbal combat.

This is a man you will probably want to crush, so try to restrain yourself. Remind yourself that you are holding back for *your* benefit, not his. If you don't stop him, you end up paying a high price for his embarrassment: it hurts you as much as it hurts him if he keeps his angry stance forever.

When someone treats you like a stereotype, you may feel a

strange pull to act like that stereotype. When a man acts paternal and treats you like a child, it is natural to respond as if he were a parent. It is difficult *not* to react the way someone expects. Be careful not to slip into the stereotype he is putting you in, but try not to overreact by acting like the direct opposite. If you do, he will still be controlling your behavior, which is what he was trying to do in the first place.

The best way to prove someone wrong when he stereotypes you is by your behavior. Just be yourself.

## Demeaning Requests

Sharon, a new VP in a software company:

> I was excited to be included in the meeting. I felt it clearly established my position in the organization. But when we all gathered in the conference room, my CEO turned to me and said, "Please bring our guest some coffee." I was the highest-ranking person in the room next to him, but I was the only woman.

What if he asks you to get the coffee? It's another way to make you seem like a girl to be discounted, rather than a professional to be reckoned with. This request and others like it—asking you to order lunch, make reservations, etc.—is a bid for power. Its goal is to show who can make who do what. He is trying to tell you that he is in control.

The most direct response, "I don't make coffee!" is the least effective. Men usually roll their eyes, look knowingly at each other, and respond condescendingly. You lose more status than you would if you brought the coffee.

One way to take control away from the man is to anticipate the attack. Offer him coffee before he has a chance to ask you to bring it. He didn't make you do anything, and you look gracious. Or plan ahead and make one of the support staff responsible for coffee.

Toni, an insurance executive, came up with a simple solution.

> Andy is always playing power games, so I was on my toes. At the beginning of an important meeting, just as we were about to begin our presentation, Andy asked me to get our clients coffee. I said, "That's a wonderful idea," and called my secretary and asked her to bring it.

If all else fails, you can take the power out of the command by responding "I'd like some, too. I'll get it for both of us." You've changed the game from bringing him coffee to getting coffee for him while you are getting it for yourself.

A technique psychologists sometimes use to calm antagonistic patients is to feed them. Try it; the power of food will surprise you. If you do get the coffee, remember you lose something, but you also gain something. The men won't know why, but they will feel good about you. Use this to your advantage.

## Flirting

JANE:

> I don't feel comfortable working with Sam. I am never sure if he thinks we are dating or working. I make it a point not to be alone with him.

JEAN:

> Sam is such a flirt. I thought he was cute and liked working with me. I was surprised and hurt when he gave the account to Herman.

These are two views of the same man. Neither view is beneficial to the speaker's career. As a weapon, flirting is extremely effective. It either seduces us, flatters us, or unnerves us because it is so offensive.

Everyone likes to think they are sexually attractive. A positive response to flirting is unconscious and automatic. If you find yourself responding to flirting, remind yourself that seductive behavior is out of place in a business setting. If the man is trying to be manipulative, he is insulting you. If he is genuinely interested in you, he can contact you after work. If he really liked and respected you, he would deal with you in a professional manner.

The easiest way to deal with flirting is to ignore it. This tells your flirtatious colleague that you are not interested, not easy to manipulate, and not overwhelmed by his charms. Of course, you can't always ignore flirting. There are times when a man's flirtatious behavior is disruptive. It can make you so angry that you have difficulty concentrating or you can find it so offensive that you avoid the man and exclude yourself from important meetings.

If you want to stop a man from flirting, ask him in a friendly, straightforward fashion if he is flirting with you. This is especially effective if you look amused. You are calling him on his game. If he denies being seductive, he will find it hard to continue to flirt without feeling foolish. If he admits to being seductive, you can tell him directly that you are not interested.

It does more harm than good to show your anger. If you sound hostile when you ask him to stop, he will have to deny flirting. He is likely to respond maliciously by muttering something about how ridiculous it would be for him to want to flirt with you. This always gets a laugh from the other men. You end up looking foolish and losing face—which is what he was trying to accomplish in the first place.

Some men are so sure of their male allure that they cannot imagine their seductive behavior would be anything but welcome. These men will not see you as a competent peer, no matter how expert you are. Don't expect such a man to respond to your subtle, or not so subtle, request that he treat you like a colleague. Be wary of this kind of man. When you don't respond to his attempts to dazzle you with his charms, you will be dealing his ego a substantial blow. If he can't overpower you by flirting, he will try another way.

There is a fine line between manipulative flirting and just being pleasant. How can you tell the difference? Observe the way he treats other men and women. Compare notes with other women who work with him. Most of all, trust your instincts.

## CHAPTER FIFTEEN

# Exclusion

This group of tactics is based on the importance that being on the Boys' Team has for men. Bill Watterson's comic strip, *Calvin and Hobbes*, illustrates this wonderfully. This comic strip is about Calvin, a little boy, and his best friend, Hobbes, an imaginary tiger. In the strip, Calvin and Hobbes are constantly finding ways to torment Susie, "a certified girl." They even form an exclusive boys' club called GROSS—Get Rid Of Stupid GirlS.[1]

When they become adults, men still try to keep women out of their clubs. Sometimes men do it overtly, by excluding women. Other times they do it more subtly, by not treating women as teammates. Each tactic in this section is a form of exclusion.

## Keeping Women Out of the Locker Room

On September, 17, 1990, Lisa Olson, a sportswriter for the *Boston Herald*, tried to do her job. She went into the New England Patriots' locker room to conduct a postgame interview. While she was interviewing Maurice Hurst at his locker, several of his teammates lewdly displayed their genitals and made suggestive comments. The rest of the team cheered them on. This abuse forced Ms. Olson out of the locker room.

Ms. Olson had invaded the most sacred of the male-only enclaves—the locker room. The Patriots' owner, Victor Kiam, defended his players. "Why not stand in front of her [naked] if she's an intruder?" proclaimed Mr. Kiam.[2]

Fortunately the NFL commissioner, Paul Tagliabue, did not agree with Mr. Kiam. After an investigation, Mr. Tagliabue levied fines totaling $22,500 against three players and ordered the club to spend $25,000 more on educational materials. But not all locker room stories have a happy ending. Many men still agree with Mr. Kiam. To them, Ms. Olson really was an intruder.

Men need the locker room and other male-only enclaves to define their identity. Little boys develop their identity as men by proving they are different from women. To prove they are different from girls, little boys sing about "greasy, grimy gopher guts." Men tell dirty jokes. The vehemence with which some men fight to keep women out of the locker room is a measure of the intensity of their need to confirm their maleness.

Ms. Olson entered a real locker room, but men treat any place from which they traditionally exclude women as a symbolic locker room. Going places and engaging in activities that exclude women are an important part of male fellowship. Men are in the symbolic locker room when they get together to play poker and drink with the boys, go on hunting and fishing trips, join fraternities and men's clubs, or stand around the water cooler talking about sports. In the locker room, men can be men. They can curse, get drunk, tell dirty jokes, and talk about their sexual conquests. As one of my sailing companions put it, the locker room is a place where men can be "crude and rude and lewd."

In the real and symbolic locker rooms, men tell dirty jokes, complain about their wives or girlfriends—and talk business. As a businesswoman, you can't afford to stay out of the locker room all the time; you will miss too much vital information. You may not enjoy being in the locker room, but you need the information. Try to join in occasionally. The men may not invite you, but they will often include you if you ask. Show up for the company softball-league game. Go out for a drink after work. Take part in the company golf tournament. Ask for company tickets to the hockey games. Learn enough about sports to join the discussion at the water cooler.

No matter how hard you try and no matter how sensitive the men, they will exclude you some of the time. Be aware that you may be missing important information. When you can't get into the locker room, try to get the information another way. Ask a male friend to keep you informed. Stay alert. Whenever you suspect there is something you don't know, ask.

I learned the dangers of not being in the locker room when I was the only woman skippering a cruise off the coast of Maine. Because navigation errors in such rocky waters can be disastrous, the skippers of the five boats in the flotilla discussed the day's route and destination each morning. One morning I watched in shock as the other four boats abruptly sailed away, leaving me behind. Luckily, I was able to gather my crew quickly and catch one of the boats. When I demanded to know why they left without telling me the float plan, the skipper retorted, "Of course you know where we are going. We all discussed it this morning in the shower."

The men's mistake created a potentially dangerous situation and a lesson I will never forget.

## Keeping Women Away from Clients and Power

Catherine, in advertising:

> In my company, travel experience is necessary for promotion. When my VP sent Joe instead of me on an impor-

tant out-of-town assignment, I asked why. He responded, "We thought you would not want to be away from your family." I asked him if he thought Joe liked being away from his family. He got the message.

Amy, an architect:

> Abe, my supervisor, casually mentioned that he and Jim, my coworker, were having dinner with a friend after work. I didn't think anything of it. The next morning I learned that this friend was an important client.

Both Catherine and Amy knew they were being denied experience essential to their advancement. Catherine's VP was keeping her at home, away from important work. Abe was inviting Jim into the old boys' network and keeping Amy out. Why?

As Margaret Mead pointed out, men have to win whenever men and women compete. They must gain and hold power. They are fighting to keep the attributes of power and prestige masculine. There is only a finite amount of power to go around. Men compete with each other for this power, but they compete with women even more. By keeping women away from places where powerful men meet and by keeping women from experiences they need to grow, men ensure that the power remains in masculine hands.

Denying women admission to the old boys' network is a very effective way to keep women away from power. The old boys' network is a loose association of acquaintances. These relationships often begin socially. Men meet in prep schools and colleges. They meet in fraternities and eating clubs. They meet in country clubs and men's clubs. They meet in the locker room of the gym.

The old boys' network is maintained both informally and formally. Men consider members of the old boys' network to be friends. They socialize with, refer business to, and help these friends. The network flourishes in organizations and places that exclude women, ranging from country clubs to professional gathering places. Men do business as well as socialize in these all-male situations. Women cannot break up the informal part of the old boys' network—you can't legislate friendships. But we can break up the institutionalized part of it.

Women are winning lawsuits against organizations that exclude them. One by one these all-male bastions are falling. The time and expense men expend to fight these lawsuits show how important this exclusivity is to men in our society. Eventually, men will lose these formal ways of excluding women, but they will always be able to do it informally. By not inviting women to informal social gatherings, men can still keep women away from power.

There is no one way to break this barrier. There is nothing subtle about excluding women from places, activities, and experiences they need to grow. It is overt and purposeful. But you can't afford to let the men exclude you. Be alert and point out each incident as it happens. If you want to succeed in your chosen profession, you need access to important clients and must tackle the kinds of assignments your company considers crucial to an executive's development. One of the best remedies to the exclusion problem is to bring it to light. Speak up and be specific about where and when you want to be included.

The demise of the old boys' network will finally occur when more power resides outside it than in it—or when the old girls' network becomes equally powerful. As women become more successful in the business world, it will become too costly for men to exclude them.

In Finland, the "sauna barrier" is the equivalent of the American locker room. Saunas are an important part of Finnish life. Even important national security debates were held in the ministry of defense's sex-segregated sauna. This practice stopped when Elizabeth Rehn became Finland's first female defense minister in 1991.

I was delighted by a March 8, 1992, article in the *Philadelphia Inquirer* that reported:

> As feminists begin devising ways of breaking into Finland's male-dominated sauna culture, Minister of Defense Rehn has discovered that she is able to commandeer the ministerial sauna from her generals any time she chooses. Last week, for example, she invited all seven female ministers in the Finnish government to join her in what used to be the inner sanctum of male power. The agenda for their discussion was not disclosed, and no one took notes.[3]

Way to go, Ms. Rehn!

## Not Helping Women

Sometimes men just won't help you. Listen to Denise, a financial analyst:

> When I joined the firm, my supervisor asked me to produce reports I had never done before. He brushed off my requests for help, telling me I was too insecure. He told me to figure them out myself. I assumed this was the culture of the firm. But when Joe joined the firm, I learned

otherwise. Joe didn't seem especially smart or competent, but he got up to speed on new work much faster than I did. I wondered what was wrong with me until I overheard my supervisor walking him through the new material step-by-step.

Men have a tradition of helping each other. In sports, a stronger player will help a weaker teammate if he is trying his best. This tradition carries over to business. But men don't always treat you, a woman, as a teammate.

Not helping you is a subtle way to undermine your competence. You can't do a job as well or as quickly if you have to reinvent the wheel every time you start a new project. By not helping you, men put you in a double bind. If you ask for help, they accuse you of insecurity. If you don't ask, they accuse you of passivity.

But occasionally, not helping you can happen inadvertently, without any hostile intentions. Men sometimes help each other during informal social conversations that take place in the "locker room."

Tim shared his frustrations about the way his wife, a banker, was mistreated:

> Harry, the senior VP, knew that Shirley was unaware of the new regulations. They weren't public yet, but she needed them to be effective in the meeting. If I realized that one of my people needed privileged information during a meeting, I would just grab him and drag him into the men's room to fill him in privately.

Then Tim realized that Harry had done just that with Norman, Shirley's coworker, but obviously not with Shirley.

If you suspect you are not getting the help you need, observe whether the male colleagues at your level get it. If they are not getting help either, it is just your corporation's culture. If they are getting it, you have to ask for it. Don't just suffer in silence, but do be careful about the way you phrase your request for help. Communicate the idea that you have tried your best. "I have done A, B, and C, but I'm not pleased with the result. Can you suggest any other approaches?" is usually effective. This tells the men that you are doing the best you can and, in the sporting tradition, they help.

If men are not helping you in the hopes you will fail, they will have excuses for not helping. The most common one is that you are much smarter than John Doe. He needed help but you obviously wouldn't. Don't buy it. Without help, you may miss a piece of vital information you had no way of finding out for yourself. There are times when a little help isn't a favor; it is essential. Ignore the excuses and demand the help. "I agree that I am smarter than John Doe, but I want your help anyway." He knows you are right. If you stand your ground, you will get the help you need.

## Ignoring What Women Say

Ruth, advertising account manager, describes a common problem:

> Phil, Joe, Sam, Arthur, and I met with the vice-president to present our new proposal. I wrote the report. Most of the important recommendations were about my products. Ernie, the VP, solicited suggestions from everyone except me. Whenever I made suggestions, I could see his eyes glaze over.

When I suggested a new plan for marketing an old product, Ernie just nodded and went on. Then Joe made the same suggestion. Everyone thought it was a wonderful idea and congratulated him for his creativity. By the time I left that meeting I was ready to quit.

Being ignored by men is the most common complaint I have heard from women. The men I interviewed willingly described many tactics they used against women, but none of them cited ignoring. This was the only tactic I asked about that men denied. Were they all lying? I don't think so. Some men dismiss women so automatically they are not aware of it.

Social psychologists who study communication find this pattern of selective inattention common in male-female interactions. Their studies show that men will attend to a woman's voice more quickly than to a man's, but they will listen more carefully to what a man has to say. For instance, if there were a fire in a movie theater, it would be most effective to have a woman yell "help" and then have a man give directions to the exit.

Other men ignore women intentionally. Being ignored has a devastating effect, whether or not it is purposeful. It makes you feel inconsequential. You start to wonder if what you have to say is important. You hesitate before contributing your ideas, wondering if they are good enough. If the group ignores your contributions, but applauds another man when he repeats them, you never get the credit or the reward for your expertise. You can't allow men to ignore you. You must counter this tactic.

When a group ignores your statement, then praises a man who echoes it, try, "Yes, I am so glad that Joe agrees with me. As I just said before . . ." and repeat your original statement. If an individual is ignoring you, ask him questions or phrase your comments as questions that require a response. "I think the green package is more effective. Don't you agree, Roger?" If he is ignoring you inadvertently, this will wake him up. If he is ignoring you purposely, he will have to respond in some manner or look foolish.

Sometimes only a face-to-face confrontation will help. Confront him *privately*, in a direct, factual way. Give specific examples, and try not to sound as hostile and angry as you probably feel. He is not likely to admit to purposely ignoring you, but if you have made your point, he is less likely to ignore you again. By confronting him privately and without hostility, you are allowing him to save face.

If he continues to ignore you, point it out again in the same calm manner. If this doesn't stop him, consider confronting him in public. This may embarrass him enough to stop him. Use this approach sparingly; it will generate a lot of hostility. Before you confront him publicly, tell him privately what you plan to do if he continues to ignore you. You are giving him fair warning. If he ignores you after your warning, call him on his behavior publicly. Show him that you will not sit back and take his abuse quietly.

A subset of ignoring is paper shuffling or loud whispering in the background. Athena, comptroller in a brewing company, shares how she responds:

> As usual, when I presented our latest reports to the board, I was the only woman in the room. In the middle of my presentation, the marketing director, Jason, began shuffling papers. Instead of trying to talk over this distracting noise, I stopped and waited for him to finish. Was his face red when he realized that everybody was staring at him!
>
> He was silent during the rest of my presentation.

Some companies are so misogynistic that the corporate culture supports ignoring women. If this is the case in your company, there is nothing you can do about it. Just don't let their behavior damage your self-esteem. If the men in your company are not going to value your skill, it is their loss. Go someplace where your expertise is valued.

## CHAPTER SIXTEEN

# Veiled Hostility

Men who use the tactics in this chapter are wolves in sheeps' clothing. In this group of tactics, men hide their hostile intent under a friendly facade. Their words may be neutral or friendly on the surface, but they still sting. These remarks are meant to hurt and to undermine your effectiveness. Some examples are:

> "Let me show you how to do it."
> "I'll carry the files. They're too heavy for you."
> "*You're* the new sales rep?"

Countering these tactics can be frustrating. Do these responses to the objections you make sound familiar?

> "I was joking. Don't you have a sense of humor?"
> "That's the thanks I get. I was only trying to help."
> "I didn't mean anything by it. You're
> oversensitive."

When men have the opportunity to respond in these ways, they are able to present themselves as the innocent, victimized party. So you need to make sure that your responses to their demeaning tactics are as veiled as the insults themselves. You won't have to specifically tell these men their tactics didn't work; they'll *know* it.

## Distractions

Julia, a trust officer:

> At our last meeting, Frank kept insisting that we had not fulfilled section three of our agreement. He went on and on. I was so intent on proving him wrong that I almost missed the changes he was trying to slip past me in section six.

Frank's attempt to distract Julia is a common tactic. He attempted to get her to focus so intently on one point that she would miss another more important point. A close cousin of this tactic is an attempt to get you angry. This often takes the form of comments muttered under the breath. The men I interviewed told me that they use this tactic on men and women, but find women more vulnerable to it.

The best way to defend yourself against this type of attack is to plan ahead. Define the problem you are trying to solve or the result you are trying to achieve specifically and concretely before you start. Know exactly what your goals are. Decide where and how much you are willing to compromise, and stick to your decision. Because you know exactly what you are trying to achieve, you can weigh every fact, argument, and offer against this goal.

Be reluctant to change your strategy midnegotiation. If you decide to change your strategy or goals after the negotiation has begun, be sure it is because you learned new facts, not because of your opponent's attempts to get you off the track. Most of the time, sticking to your original well-thought-out plan is the best way to go.

A useful habit to get into is to make a brief outline of your negotiation points. Aim for one page or less. You will always have the most important points right in front of you. Your outline will keep you to the point. If your opponent tries to distract you, mark the point you were trying to make when the frivolous objection or irrelevant discussion started. When the distraction is over, you can easily start where you left off. This way, you won't miss any essential points.

## Offers of Help

Sarah, a biochemist:

> Tully loudly offered to show me how to write the new report. But I knew he wasn't trying to be helpful. He *couldn't* be. He didn't know any more than I did. He was just trying to make me look bad.

How can you call someone hostile when he is trying to help you? Easily, when he is using his offer of help to belittle you. We can all use a little help, but before you accept it, ask yourself who it will really benefit. Sincere help is always welcome, but an offer of help can also be an insult. "You don't know how to do that, do you? Let me show you."

Don't take help if it is offered in a condescending or hostile way. Find out what you need to know quietly from another source. Never take help from an opponent. He is the last person you should trust. "Let me show you how to use the computer" can really mean "I want your password so I can steal your accounts."

If you really need help and there is nowhere else to get it, swallow your pride and take it. But be sure the help is correct. Remember, men like to pretend they know how to do everything and be the experts. I have seen men who had no idea what they were doing "helping" and thereby causing a great deal of harm.

Demi, a biologist, told me this story:

> I was walking past Juanita's desk and overheard her ask Burt how to exit a computer program she was unfamiliar with. He told her to exit without saving her report because the program had an "auto-save" feature. I use the same program and knew his advice was wrong. I stopped her just in time. Then Burt admitted that he never used that program. He just assumed the program would save Juanita's work when she exited.

## Condescending Remarks

"You just don't understand things like this."
"Not bad for a girl."
"What are *you* doing in this meeting?"

Condescending remarks are direct attacks. They don't deserve the respect of a response. The best response to a condescending remark is silence. You can prove it untrue in the context of your work. If you react to condescending remarks, you are guaranteed to hear a lot more of them in the future.

Pat yourself on the back when someone speaks to you condescendingly. He is condescending because he knows you are more effective than he is. He is trying to belittle you because your competence frightens him. By ignoring his condescending remarks, you force him to deal with you as a professional—which is exactly what he is trying to avoid.

It's hard not to respond to an insult. When you are in danger of losing your temper, remember this: A man makes condescending remarks because he thinks you are too formidable to deal with in a professional manner. Consider it a compliment.

## Biting Humor

Molly, a neurologist:

> I hate when Alphonse makes snide remarks. When I ask him to stop, he feigns surprise, saying, "Don't be so serious. I was only kidding."

Almost any insult can be cloaked in a joke. Most of the time you can easily tell if the humor is hostile or friendly, but on occasion, the motivation of the joker is unclear.

If you are unsure about the motivation behind a joke, ask. When a remark offends you, say so. If the joker was not trying to hurt you, he will apologize. We all miscommunicate or make thoughtless remarks on occasion. If the joke was hostile, the man will defend himself, as Alphonse did.

Men like Alphonse are difficult to deal with verbally. The more you say, the more he will make fun of you—especially if he has an audience. If his jokes sting, don't let him know. Molly finally stopped Alphonse by using a nonverbal response. When she began thinking of him as an overgrown adolescent, her look of amused disdain stopped him cold.

Men and women use humor differently. This difference causes miscommunication. Men use humor as a way to connect as well as a way to hurt. They connect with each other by rough-housing, backslapping, and wrestling. When they can't fight physically, they hit each other with rough verbal humor.

Men enjoy bantering. Throwing escalating insults at each other is a frequent male game. A man who is trying to be friendly may include you in this game. He means his remarks to be funny, not hurtful. He doesn't expect you to take them seriously. He thinks you know that they don't reflect his real feelings about you.

Don't misinterpret these remarks as hostile. If you enjoy bantering, join in. If you don't enjoy the game, tell him so. Men who are trying to be friendly will stop. Any man who won't stop, like Alphonse, is not your friend, in business or otherwise.

## Irrelevant Personal Questions

Some questions have no purpose but to distract or upset you:

> "Just how old are you anyway?"
> "Are you married?"
> "How long have you been practicing?"

Irrelevant personal questions, like your age or your marital status, are on the line where insults end and sexual harassment begins. You don't have to answer these questions. A way to deflect them is to ask calmly, "What's that relevant to?" or "Why are you asking me that?" This will clarify the man's motivation.

Men who are using these questions as a form of harassment usually produce a transparent excuse for asking them. "Uh . . . I wanted to know how old you were because I know someone who might be your age who you might have met." Once you hear them, it is best to let these pale excuses go by. You have successfully given him the message that he can't unnerve you this way.

## Exploiting Women's Nurturing Tendencies

Some men exploit women's soft, nurturing side. Our culture socializes women to be caretakers. Women learn not to hurt anyone. Most women are more comfortable giving than taking, trusting than tricking. These are positive feminine traits that you wouldn't want to change. But these positive traits become vulnerabilities when they are used against you.

> "There goes Doug with his girls," Christina said with a sigh as we walked down the hall to her office. "I try to warn the young MBAs, but they won't listen. They think Doug is amiable and fatherly, so they'll do anything he wants. They don't realize he has no intention of promoting any of them. He's just using them to make himself look good. I know. I used to be one of them. I had to leave the department to get ahead."

Most organizations have men like Doug in their ranks. Doug gets the glory while his assistants toil quietly in the background. He tells his assistants he is lobbying for their promotions, but he isn't. He wants to keep them working for him as long as possible. Doug looks for women who have been raised to be helpmates and takes advantage of them. Rather than encourage their growth, he encourages their dependence.

Too many women are comfortable working hard in the background, expecting to be rewarded for their good work. They won't be. To advance in the workplace you need recognition. Don't let yourself be manipulated this way. You can help your coworkers and support your supervisors. Just be sure to get the credit you deserve.

Lawrence preys on women slightly differently. Colette told me:

> I mustered my courage and asked Lawrence for a raise. He had the most hurt look on his face. "Don't you think I'd give you a raise as soon as we are making more money?" he said. I backed down quickly, feeling guilty. Then I learned that he had just given Matthew a raise the week before.

Lawrence knows women don't like to hurt anyone. By looking hurt, he easily gets his way. If Lawrence can't get what he wants by looking hurt, he feigns anger. He knows women don't want to make anyone angry either. Be sure you are being treated fairly and evenhandedly. If you back down every time someone looks hurt or angry, soon you will be losing every battle.

I'm not suggesting you become insensitive or coldhearted. Don't ignore your empathy or compassion. Just don't let them become weapons to be used against you.

## CHAPTER SEVENTEEN

# Scare Tactics

Men who use scare tactics are bullies. They use scare tactics to rattle you. Men yell, curse, act angry, and use their physical presence to frighten you. They hope you will give up, accede to their demands, or become so unnerved that you make mistakes.

Men do not reserve scare tactics for women. They use them on each other as well. No man likes it when someone yells at him, but men have had practice yelling and being yelled at. Men shout at each other while playing sports. It is traditional for managers of sports teams to lose their tempers and threaten the referees, even though the managers get penalized for it.

Men learn to tolerate the bullying and remain unscathed. You can learn to do the same. Remember your strengths. Men use these tactics because they cannot beat you on a level playing field. They fear your competence. If you do not let these threats rattle you, your skill will prevail.

## Yelling

Augusta, marketing consultant:

> My department head, Jerome, wants us to consider everyone's input and make joint decisions—unless he

wants something *his* way. He doesn't discuss then; he yells. Jerome thinks if he just shouts louder and louder, I will quietly go away.

Some men, like Jerome, will try to frighten you by yelling. They want to frighten you into acceding to their demands. It is hard not to feel frightened when someone shouts at you. That is what the shouting is meant to accomplish. If you feel frightened, don't let it show. When a man starts to yell, take a deep breath and keep your composure.

It helps to think of the bellowing man as a child having a temper tantrum. An adult male would be talking, not shouting. Treat him as you would treat a child. If you respond to a child's tantrum, the child will have a tantrum whenever he wants something. If you ignore him, he will eventually stop crying. When you ignore a bellowing man, he eventually stops yelling.

However, you can't always ignore yelling. Sometimes you need an active method to stop the yelling. Luanne, a labor negotiator, told me that when a man shouts at her over the phone, she quietly hangs up. Then she calls the person back immediately, pretending they were inadvertently disconnected. The other person knows she really hung up, but can't prove it. If he was truly angry, he has had a moment to cool off. If he was shouting to be manipulative, he knows it won't work.

Some people find speaking very softly effective when other people are yelling. Eventually the others stop yelling and listen. In a face-to-face encounter, body language is an effective tool. With your facial expression and posture, you can look bored, amused, disgusted, or maternal. Not only can you let him and any audience know you are not afraid, you can make him look foolish rather than powerful.

Most of the time, yelling back is counterproductive. Shouting back may escalate the situation. But yelling back can be effective in special situations. If you use it cautiously and sparingly, it is like a splash of cold water.

Charlene, who works for the manager of a professional sports team, has been in a situation where speaking quietly is useless. She offered a suggestion for handling a loudmouth who just keeps drowning you out and ignoring you:

> In this sports culture, he who yells the loudest, wins. Rocky will yell over me if I talk quietly. But if I keep raising my voice to match his, he will quiet down. It's a game. It doesn't matter what I say, I just have to hold my ground.

Don't let anyone intimidate you with his anger or noise. Clamor is the weapon of an insecure man. He is more frightened of you than you will ever be of him.

## Acting Angry

Germaine, VP of public relations:

> I thought Dave would explode when the printer told him the proofs weren't ready. When we walked out, I began trying to cool Dave off. He surprised me by saying perfectly calmly, "Didn't you know I was faking? I want the printer to remember me, for next time."

Men know the power of anger. Anger implies the threat of force. We respond viscerally, even when we know there is no physical danger. Anger is so potent that men will fake it if they think it will be effective.

Men use anger to influence each other—as Dave was doing. But anger is an especially effective weapon against women. Because most men are physically bigger, their anger feels more frightening to a woman. Men know this. They also know that women have been trained to please and to soothe angry people. Men hope that you will want to calm them down rather than fight back.

You have to decide whether the most effective response is to fight back or to soothe. If it is a conflict in which you want to fight back, don't let the anger stop you. It doesn't matter if the anger is feigned or real, it can't hurt you. How likely is he to attack you physically? Confront your fear. Resist the impulse to maintain peace at all costs. You have more to lose by giving in than by standing your ground.

## Physical Presence

Nina, a trainer in a large management consulting firm:

> I hate working with Arnold. He's so big. When we disagree, he makes it a point to stand close and tower over me. I feel like a child when I argue with someone who is looking down at the top of my head.

Beverly, an architect:

> I have a similar problem giving presentations with Dino. He's six-one; I'm five-two. People respond as if he's more powerful than I am. They show him more respect than they show me. He makes a point to magnify the differences in our sizes by standing close to me.

You can't change your size, but you can keep it from being a liability. Your size can affect how others perceive you. People do perceive the bigger person as more powerful. And it does feel uncomfortable when someone towers over you. Big men use their size to their advantage with other men, but it often functions even better against women.

You can keep a man from using his size against you. In an argument, try not to let a large man stand close or lean over you. It feels threatening to have a large man looming over you and yelling. If you have to negotiate with a large man, try to make him sit down as soon as possible. If sitting isn't possible, stand as far away as you reasonably can. The closer you are, the sharper the angle between your eyes. When you stand at a distance, this evens out a bit.

Pay attention to your body language. You will feel and look stronger if you stand straight and make eye contact. Keep your voice strong and level. Choose your words carefully and speak definitively. If you stand your ground, your competence will overwhelm his bulk.

## Cursing

Monica, owner of a catering service, described a conversation with one of her suppliers:

> When I didn't agree to his terms, he called me a f--king bitch. Nobody ever called me that before. Does he think I will be afraid to disagree with him again? I hope I never have to deal with him again—but if I do, I'll have a tape recorder with me.

Cursing is rude behavior. The man cursing at you is purposely being rude to you or is a crude person in general. Either way, he is not a threat; he is just a boor.

For some men, swearing is a part of their everyday language. They are at a loss for words to replace the curses. These men think there is something wrong with you if you object to their language and will use your complaints as a reason not to work with you. But most men know that cursing is offensive to most women.

Cursing is an explicit attempt to be intimidating. The less you respond to cursing meant to unnerve you, the less men will use it against you—why bother if it doesn't work? You don't have to use foul language yourself, just don't let it intimidate you.

Some cursing is inevitable in primarily male workplaces. Men curse to prove their masculinity to other men as well as to women. The amount of cursing that men consider appropriate varies with the kind of work and the corporate culture. In traditional "macho" occupations, like trucking or construction, cursing is part of the vocabulary. If you want to work in a field like this, you have to develop some tolerance for foul language.

Depending on our backgrounds, we have different thresholds for swearing. No matter how high your threshold, there is a point when swearing becomes too abusive and should be stopped.

You can embarrass some men into stopping if you keep a straight face and very politely say, "I'm sorry, I couldn't hear you. Would you repeat that?" Rarely will a man repeat his curse. Most become uncomfortable. Men also feel embarrassed or belittled if you can look maternally, condescendingly amused. You make him feel like a guilty schoolboy.

Let a crude man know that you don't want anyone speaking to you so disrespectfully, but you are not going to lose your composure because of his language. Any man whose best attack at you is a coarse word is not strong enough or smart enough to be concerned about.

## Verbal Combat

Scare tactics are terrorist tactics. Men who use them are attempting to be so intimidating that you retreat rather than fight for what you want. Standing your ground against an angry, unreasonable man is not easy. The more confident you are in your ability to hold your own in a fight, the easier it becomes.

Verbal combat is a skill you can learn. Experts at doing verbal battle—debaters, politicians, interviewers, negotiators, lawyers, and talk-show hosts—are masters at verbal sparring techniques. You can learn these techniques, too. Take every opportunity to observe experts. Media interviews, especially of politicians, provide many good examples of these techniques. Recognize when they are being used against you. Experiment. Practice using verbal sparring techniques. Pay attention to how you feel when you do so, and how your opponent reacts.

The more your confidence increases, the less vulnerable you will feel.

### A. Don't Make Him Any More Defensive Than He Is

There is no reasoning with someone who is on the defensive. By carefully phrasing your questions and statements in terms of your own feelings, rather than accusatory statements, you have the best chance of getting a positive response.

When you want someone to act differently, try using the following phrases to express yourself:[1]

| | |
|---|---|
| When you . . . | (describe the behavior) |
| The effects are . . . | (describe the effects in specific, concrete terms) |
| I feel . . . | (express what you think and feel) |
| I'd prefer . . . | (specify the behavior you would like) |
| The result will be . . . | (describe the consequences of making or not making the requested change) |

Here are two examples:

| | |
|---|---|
| When you . . . | ask me to complete a huge assignment in two hours. |
| The effects are . . . | I am not able to do a thorough job. |
| I feel . . . | frustrated when I cannot do my best. |
| I'd prefer . . . | that you give me more lead time. |
| The result will be . . . | I can produce a better product with more lead time. |

| | |
|---|---|
| When you . . . | shout. |
| The effects are . . . | I am not able to hear your comments. |

| | |
|---|---|
| I feel . . . | frustrated because I cannot answer your complaints. |
| I'd prefer . . . | that you express your concerns calmly. |
| The result will be . . . | I will address your concerns when you speak calmly. When you shout, I am going to leave the room until you calm down. |

## B. Try to Bring His Attention Back to the Issue and Away from the Emotion

Refocusing someone's attention has a calming effect. It helps everyone to think more clearly. Here are several ways to do this:

1. Try to postpone the conversation until everyone is cool.

    example: I'll be happy to discuss this with you when you are calmer. Let's talk about this later when we have more time. Can you meet with me at two?

2. Calmly repeat the speaker's words. Hearing himself being unreasonable may wake him up and calm him down.

    example: You are angry that the fifty-page report you gave me an hour ago is not complete. You think I am a total idiot who never completes any assignments on time.

3. Ask questions. Occasionally, you will uncover a misunderstanding. Even if you don't, forcing him to interrupt his tirade to answer your questions will calm him down. It interrupts the tirade and forces him to think rationally.

> example: The specs say the report is due tomorrow. Was there a change? Why do you want the report today? Is the deadline irrevocable? What will happen if you get it tomorrow? Who could work on this report besides me?

4. Stay with one thought. People often get off the track when they are upset. They bring unrelated, but emotional, issues into the conversation. Keep the conversation on track. Insist on resolving one issue at a time.

> example: Let's not talk about who has seniority. That has nothing to do with this account. I would like to know why you returned the call rather than give me the phone messages.

5. Agree with something your opponent says and then go on to make your point. The point you agree with does not have to be related to the point you are going to make. Because you are agreeing with

him, you sound more reasonable to your opponent. He is more likely to listen to your point.

example: I agree that your format is the best one for this report. I think points three, four, and five should be . . .

6. Use repetition.
   a. Respond *briefly* to any legitimate points made by the other person while repeating your point. Make your point, respond to any reasonable objections, and then make your point again.

   example: I think Felice is the best person to do the job. She knows the material better than anyone else. Yes, Tammi has been here longer, but Felice is more knowledgeable about this issue.

   b. Selectively ignore the points that are not favorable to you. Ignore any criticism or questions. Just keep making your point. This is a favorite of politicians being interviewed on news shows.

   example: The point I want to make is that Felice is the best person for the job, knows the most about the issue, and is clearly the choice of the majority of the people she will have to work with. There is no doubt in my mind she can do the job.

## C. Don't Accept No for an Answer

If you don't succeed the first time, ask again, and again, and again. Some people answer no automatically before they even consider the merits of the request. More requests are granted on the second and third tries than on the first.

Don't be afraid to be a pest. Be a pest. Be a nag. Be a squeaky wheel. It works.

# Sexual Harassment and Sex Discrimination

Stacy, financial planner:

> I quit my job because my boss was sexually harassing me.
> He threatened to write a poor evaluation if I didn't sleep
> with him. I didn't and he did. I was afraid that if I pressed
> the issue, I would be blackballed from the industry.

Maxine, account manager for a national real-estate company:

> There were four regional managers in my area before
> my company decided to consolidate the area into one
> region. They transferred the three male managers to
> managerial positions in different areas and left me here.
> Then they brought in another man to run the region
> and supervise me. I'm far more experienced and quali-
> fied than he is to run the region. The VP said his gut in-
> stincts were that this man had the stuff to do the job
> and I didn't. I have to decide whether I want to leave or
> file a complaint and fight.

Jill, stockbroker:

> These are grown men, but they act like adolescents. Nude
> calendars on the walls, dirty sexual remarks and gestures
> when I walk into the room, insinuations about how I got
> my job. Nothing I said made them stop. When Harry
> graphically described what he wanted to do to me and the
> others clapped, I got really frightened. I filed a complaint.
> I haven't received a good assignment since.

Doris, graphic designer:

> There are no women in upper management in my com-
> pany—and sure enough, they denied my request for a
> promotion. My supervisor said that my skills aren't good
> enough, and added that I'm abrasive, aggressive, and
> have poor people skills. He also mentioned that I took
> time off for maternity leave. Men with less skill, who are
> downright rude and more aggressive than I will ever be,
> are routinely promoted. Hans, who was promoted when
> I was passed over, took more time off for the flu last year
> than I did for maternity leave. I'm suing.

Sexual harassment and sex discrimination are serious problems
for women in the workplace today. As more women reach higher
levels in the workforce, these problems are likely to get worse before they get better. Why do men sexually harass women? What
motivates a company to practice sex discrimination? What if it
happens to you?

Sexual harassment and sex discrimination are driven by the
same motive: the need for power. In sexual harassment, sex is
the weapon men use to frighten, intimidate, and manipulate
women. In sex discrimination, men use their administrative

power to deny women employment or advancement just because they are women. The fewer women advanced, the more power left for the men.

Sexual harassment is the ugliest tactic men use against women. In the scare tactics I wrote about in the previous chapter, men threaten violence. Sexual harassment *is* violence. It is about power, not sex. Sex is just the weapon these men use to overpower and humiliate women.

Sexual harassment is as monstrous, as painful, and as damaging a crime as rape. Like rape victims, victims of sexual harassment are blamed for their own victimization. In both crimes, women who try to prosecute are likely to be doubly victimized: first by the harasser and then by the legal process. Like rape, sexual harassment takes an enormous psychological toll on its victims.

Victims of sexual harassment suffer emotional trauma similar to rape victims. They feel depressed, anxious, guilty, and humiliated. Their self-esteem plummets. They are haunted by nightmares about the harassment. Dr. Mary P. Koss, professor of psychiatry at the University of Arizona Medical School, has studied sexual aggression and victimization among the general population for over fifteen years.[1] Her research shows that because sexual harassment usually continues over a period of time and involves people you are supposed to trust, the emotional consequences can be even more severe and long lasting than rape.

Many sexually harassed women suffer from post-traumatic stress disorder, the same malady that afflicts Vietnam veterans and earthquake survivors.[2] Survivors of these traumas suffer from recurrent, intrusive, and distressing recollections and dreams of the event. They often feel intense anxiety when they are exposed to situations that resemble or symbolize the traumatic events and attempt to avoid situations, thoughts, feelings, conversations, places, or people that remind them of the trauma. They feel anxious, irritable, jumpy, and angry. Some victims feel a general numbness or detachment from others. Post-traumatic stress disorder is not only painful, it makes functioning at home and at work extremely difficult.

Our culture encourages women to blame themselves when they are sexually harassed. Our society insinuates that it is a woman's responsibility to control a man's sexuality. In cases of sexual harassment, as in cases of date rape, the victimizer may claim that he was sure the women liked his behavior, that she didn't protest enough, or that she instigated it.

Unfortunately, some women buy into this idea. Sexual harassment victims often feel guilty and responsible. They wonder what they did to cause the harassment. If you are being sexually harassed, it is because you are a woman, not because of anything you did or didn't do. If you are being sexually harassed, *it is not your fault.*

When Anita Hill faced the Senate subcommittee to testify about her experiences with Clarence Thomas, she changed the lives of many women and raised the consciousness of a country. She deserves our gratitude and our respect. After Ms. Hill's testimony, women who had been sexually harassed began speaking up. Men and women who had observed sexual harassment began talking about it. The country stopped denying that sexual harassment was a problem in the workplace. Social scientists have long suspected that sexual harassment was an underreported crime, but until Anita Hill opened the floodgates, they never realized how underreported it was. The Equal Employment Opportunity Commission reported that in the three-month period following the Hill-Thomas hearings, its offices nationwide received 1,244 complaints of sexual harassment. In comparison, during the same months the year before, the agency recorded 728 complaints.

Numerous women who never admitted being sexually harassed began to talk about their experiences. They had been reluctant to speak up for a variety of reasons. They were afraid that no one would believe them. They were not sure if their experience was *really* sexual harassment. They were afraid of repercussions. Some had tried to tell someone in their company and had been ignored, accused of lying, or punished. Others had won grievances but didn't want anyone to know for fear they would be labeled as troublemakers.

The statistics from recent surveys of sexual harassment take your breath away. In 1981, the *Harvard Business Review* reported the results of a survey of 7,408 managers. Sexual harassment had occurred in 63 percent of these companies.[3] In 1989, a survey of Fortune 500 companies showed that 90 percent had received complaints of sexual harassment. Thirty-four percent of these companies had been sued. Companies with clear antiharassment policies reported that 95 percent of the complaints they received were judged valid.[4]

Most people assume that sexual harassment happens primarily in blue-collar occupations, or only to low-level staff, or only to unsophisticated women. This is not the case. In 1990, the Young Lawyers Division of the American Bar Association asked female lawyers if they had experienced or observed sexual harassment. Eighty-five percent of the women said yes.[5] In the same year, a study reported in the *Journal of the American Medical Association* concluded that 55 percent of the female medical students surveyed had experienced some degree of sexual harassment at work.[6] *No class of workers is immune. Any woman can be a target.*

The stereotype of the harasser as a man who is clumsy in his attempts to date women is just that—a stereotype, not a reality. Sexual harassment is usually part of a pattern of abusive behavior. Most harassers have left a string of abused women behind them. Men who harass feed their need for power and try to overcome their sense of insecurity at the expense of others. Some sexual harassers are crude men. They think sexually offensive behavior is the normal way to relate to women. Others are misogynists. They are angry at women, see them as competitors, and resent women's presence in the workplace. A crude man may stop if you confront him early and explicitly tell him that his behavior is offensive, wrong, and illegal. Nothing you say will stop the misogynist. He is out for blood.

Victims of sexual harassment or sex discrimination had no legal recourse until 1964. Sex discrimination was included in the groundbreaking Civil Rights Act of 1964. In the 1960s, when this act was written, the country's focus was on racial discrimination. The clause about sex discrimination was included almost as an afterthought.

Title VII of the 1964 Civil Rights Act makes it illegal for businesses to hire, discriminate against, or limit employees in any way that could hurt their status because of race, color, religion, sex, or national origin. The act did not explicitly mention sexual harassment. In 1980, the Equal Employment Opportunity Commission (EEOC) developed very specific guidelines for sexual harassment. In 1986, the Supreme Court ruled that sexual harassment is sex discrimination barred by Title VII of the Civil Rights Act. Since then, the EEOC has received about five thousand sexual harassment complaints annually.

The EEOC guidelines are very important because they are the definition of sexual harassment used by the courts.

Sexual harassment, as defined by the EEOC[7] (the words that follow in italics are my additions, not part of the Act), is:

> Any unwelcome sexual advances, requests for sexual favors, or other verbal or physical conduct of a sexual nature constitutes sexual harassment when

i.  submission to such conduct is made either explicitly or implicitly a term or condition of an individual's employment *(Sleep with me if you want the job)*,

ii. submission to or rejection of such conduct by an individual is used as the basis for employment decisions affecting such individual *(Sleep with me if you want a promotion)*, or

iii. such conduct has the purpose or effect of unreasonably interfering with an individual's work performance or creating an intimidating, hostile or offensive working environment *(Pornographic pictures on the walls, graphic dirty jokes at your expense, lewd remarks, generally abusive behavior).*

The EEOC divides sexual harassment into two categories: quid pro quo harassment and hostile-working-environment harassment. Quid pro quo means something given in exchange for something else. Stacy's complaint at the beginning of this chapter is an example of quid pro quo harassment: her boss tried to blackmail her by threatening to deny her a good evaluation if she did not have sex with him.

Hostile-working-environment harassment occurs when a person is tormented by unwelcome sexual advances, intimidation, hostility, or offensive behavior at work. Jill's experience with dirty remarks and insinuations from her coworkers is an example of this.

Hostile-working-environment harassment is more subjective than quid pro quo harassment and harder to prove. Because people differ in their definition of offensive behavior, our legal system developed the "reasonable woman" standard. The harassing behavior has to be offensive to a "reasonable women." To qualify as hostile-working-environment harassment, the behavior has to be pervasive and repetitive. One occurrence is not enough unless it is extraordinarily vile.

Very often people disagree on just what is or isn't sexual harassment. Studies show that men and women differ in their definitions of offensive behavior.[8] Women consider more behaviors offensive than men do. Women also differ among themselves. Everyone can agree that repugnant behaviors, like cornering a woman in a closet and groping her, or a man exposing himself, are sexual harassment. But what about sexist comments about women's behavior, crude sexual remarks, leering, displaying pornography, sexual innuendos, or propositions? These behaviors all qualify as sexual harassment if they meet the pervasive and repetitive standard, but women are far more likely to identify them as sexual harassment than men.

Sexual harassment is *any* unwelcome sexual advances, *any* unwanted propositions, *any* offensive verbal or physical contact. If you ask someone to stop an offensive behavior and he doesn't, you are being harassed. Title VII gives you the right to work in an environment that is not intimidating, hostile, or offensive. If you are intimidated or offended by someone or something of a sexual nature in your environment, and he refuses to make the reasonable changes you request, you are being harassed.

You can't ignore sexual harassment. It won't just go away. Ignoring is the best way to deal with some of the tactics men use against women. If you don't respond, the men stop. *Not so with sexual harassment.* It is the one tactic you should *never* ignore. You must confront it.

Most people's first response to sexual harassment is to try to explain it away. "He was only joking." "Boys will be boys." "He's having a hard time at home." The people around you will be glad to help you rationalize it, because most people would prefer not to deal with it.

But nobody has the right to hurt you. If you are being sexually harassed, the harassment is probably eroding your self-esteem and sense of self-worth. Women who are sexually harassed commonly feel isolated, hopeless, helpless, and demoralized. That is how the harasser wants you to feel. It's hard to fight when you feel hopeless, but fighting is essential for your well-being. If you are being sexually harassed:

1. Talk to someone you trust. Talk to a friend, a significant other, a coworker. Do not suffer in silence. You will need emotional support to keep going. Silence helps the harasser. He is free to harass woman after woman, none of them necessarily knowing about each other.

2. Tell the harasser in no uncertain terms to stop. Tell him his attentions are unwanted. Be clear, direct, explicit. "I will not have sex with you. Do not ask me again." "Take your hand off my breast and do not touch me again." "Calling me a c--t is offensive, stop it."

3. Keep a diary of the offending behavior. This is very important. Make notes as soon after the harassing incident as you can. You can keep a separate book or just make notes in your appointment book. This ensures that you remember the details. These notes may be admissible as evidence in court if they are made at the time of the incidents.

4. If the harasser does not stop, use your company's grievance procedure, if there is one. Most large companies have a step-by-step process. The first step is usually informing your supervisor or the affirmative action specialist in your company's human relations department. Most grievance procedures allow you to bypass your supervisor if he is the harasser.

5. If your company has no formal grievance procedure, talk to your supervisor, or his supervisor, or any high-level person in your company's hierarchy.

6. The supervisor or grievance committee should investigate. Expect to be interviewed and questioned. Most cases are resolved at this point.

7. If you are not satisfied with your employer's response or the harassment does not stop, report the harassment to the EEOC or your state's civil rights or human relations department. State and federal laws differ. Depending on where you live, filing with one agency may be more beneficial to you than the other. You will find the EEOC listed in the phone book. Call them and follow their procedure to the letter.

8. If you want to file a complaint with the EEOC or are considering a lawsuit, you must act quickly. The statute of limitations is brief. The average is just 180 days. It begins to run when the harassment starts. DO NOT WAIT.

9. If you are a government employee, go to your administrative affirmative action officer. You must go through proper channels and follow government procedures to the letter.

10. TALK TO AN ATTORNEY WHO SPECIALIZES IN SEXUAL HARASSMENT. I recommend doing this early in the process. Sexual harassment cases are so hard to prove, you can't afford to make mistakes. The law and common sense are not always the same thing.

Now let's focus on sex discrimination. Once again, Title VII of the 1964 Civil Rights Act makes it illegal for businesses to hire, discriminate against, or limit employees in any way that can hurt the employee's status because of race, color, religion, sex, or national origin. Treating women differently just because they are women is a clear violation of this act. It is sex discrimination when a company pays women less than men in similar positions, does not promote women, denies women the opportunities necessary for advancement, or does not hire women who are qualified.

In cases of sex discrimination, the men who make the hiring and advancement decisions use their administrative power to keep women in their place—behind the men. Maxine and Doris, whose stories are at the beginning of this chapter, are victims of sex discrimination. Maxine's company replaced her as regional manager and Doris's company denied her a promotion just because they are women.

Like victims of sexual harassment, victims of sex discrimination feel helpless, hopeless, powerless, anxious, depressed, and demoralized. At points, they question their own judgment. They know they are being discriminated against unfairly, but the men in power consistently deny it. These men justify their actions with vague excuses. Most victims of sex discrimination feel confused and unsure about what is happening to them at first.[9]

The discriminators deny conversations that took place or claim they had conversations that never happened. The work you thought was excellent is suddenly criticized. Supervisors find faults where there are none. Your interpersonal skills, which have always served you well, are suddenly labeled inadequate. You are told you are abrasive, lack diplomacy, are passive, unprofessional, or ineffective. When this happens to them, some women describe a sense of unreality—it's like being in the Twilight Zone.

If you think you are a victim of sex discrimination, talk to someone you trust. You need the clear vision of an outsider to restore your confidence in your own judgment. Sometimes the discrimination is so blatant that you have no doubt it is sex discrimination, but you feel powerless to change it. In other cases, your employer makes you doubt your judgment and begin to wonder if you are oversensitive or misreading the situation. It is easy to fall into the trap of believing that the discrimination is your fault. Before you can do anything to stop the discrimination, you must be very clear in your own mind that you are being unfairly discriminated against because of gender.

If you think you are a victim of sex discrimination:

1. Evaluate your situation critically from as many angles as you can. Be very sure that you are being discriminated against and the discrimination is because of gender. Ask yourself:

   a. Are you being treated differently from your male counterparts? If possible, ask a coworker you trust for his or her opinion.

   b. Are you being treated differently because you are a woman? Could there be any other reason you are being treated differently?

   c. Are your male and female coworkers being treated differently from you? If so, in what ways?

   d. Are you receiving the same criticism from others? If not, whose judgment do you value more? If others are saying you are doing a good job, you probably are.

   e. Could it be true that you are not doing your job well? Do an honest self-assessment of your work.

2. When you are being criticized, ask for facts, documents, details, and specific incidents. In most cases of sex discrimination, the criticisms are vague and subjective and there are no documents.

3. Keep a diary. Make a note of every conversation you think is evidence of sex discrimination right af-

ter the conversation. The more details you remember, the better.

4. Some states have laws that require an employer to show an employee her personnel file if she asks. If this is the case in your state (check with the EEOC), consider looking at it.

   a. How do your present evaluations stack up against past evaluations?

   b. Is there anything in this file you didn't know about?

5. If there is a company policy or procedure for dealing with sex discrimination, use it. It is worth a try, but don't rely on it as the sole source of help.

6. If you are not satisfied with your company's response to your complaint, file a complaint with the EEOC or your state civil rights or human relations department. Act quickly, the statute of limitations varies from state to state. It is usually very short and begins as soon as you learn of the discrimination.

7. If you are a government employee, talk to your administrative affirmative action officer. You must go through proper channels and follow government procedures to the letter.

8. TALK TO AN ATTORNEY WHO SPECIALIZES IN SEX DISCRIMINATION LITIGATION IMMEDIATELY. Consulting an attorney does not mean you have to litigate. An attorney can help you understand your rights and help you decide whether or not you want to bring a suit. An attorney can advise you, help you negotiate with your employer, or negotiate for you.

Sexual harassment and sex discrimination in the workplace are intolerable. These practices must be stopped. By speaking up in any way, you are helping to end these practices. If you suffer in silence, you help keep these practices alive. Fortunately, the fear of lawsuits is forcing employers to reexamine the way they treat women.

Sexual harassment and sex discrimination lawsuits are very ugly. A lawsuit will take an enormous toll on you.[10] It will be emotionally draining. It will hurt your professional reputation and make doing your job more difficult. I have tremendous respect for women with the courage and stamina to go through with their suits. Not all of us have that capacity.

Deciding whether or not to sue is a difficult, and a personal, decision. Every person and every situation is different. There is no one right answer for everyone. Most cases settle without trials; they are resolved within the company or with the EEOC. But some employers will fight to the end. So don't be hard on yourself if you decide that a lawsuit is too painful or too frightening for you. Your fears are valid. No matter how the suit turns out, you will be put through an emotional wringer. Even if you win, you may find it impossible to stay at your job. Other employers in your field may be reluctant to hire you. If there is an amicable way to resolve your dispute, use it. You deserve considerable credit for acknowledging the problem and trying to stop it.

Women are an important part of the workforce today and will become even more important in the future. No company can afford to lose their competent women. If you cannot stop the harassment or discrimination, leave. Work for a company that respects you and appreciates your talents. Don't use your expertise to help foster the growth of a misogynistic company. A steady stream of competent women leaving a company will deprive that company of vital talent. It also helps the women who decide to sue by reinforcing their claim that the company is unfriendly to women. Take the path that is best for you.

We can eliminate sex harassment and sex discrimination from the workplace by not tolerating these practices. Ignoring or pretending the problem isn't there allows sex discrimination and sexual harassment to thrive. If you are being sexually harassed or are a victim of sex discrimination, *do something about it.* Enlist the support of your close friends. Talk with a competent attorney. You can try to change your company's system, you can change jobs, or you can sue.

You are a valuable human being. You deserve to be treated with respect and compensated for your abilities. Silence and passivity allow sexual harassment and sex discrimination to flourish. If every woman stands up to sexual harassment and sex discrimination, we will put an end to these practices.

## CHAPTER NINETEEN

# Where Do We Go from Here?

*Even though you are on the right track, you'll get run over if you just stay there.*

—WILL ROGERS

Women today can feel proud of the strides they have made in the workplace. A 1993 census of female directors compiled by the research organization Catalyst showed that more than half of the Fortune 1000 companies now have female directors, usually one per board.[1] In 1983, executive search firm Korn/Ferry found that only 41 percent of these companies had women on their boards, and that in 1973, only 11 percent included women. Forty-four percent of adult working women are college-educated, compared with only 20 percent in 1965. Women now receive over half of all master's degrees and one third of all doctorates.[2]

But 97 percent of senior managers at the Fortune 1000 corporations are still white males. Even though 57 percent of the workforce is female, only 5 percent of the top managers at Fortune 2000 companies are women.[3] Women still earn less than men in every job category. The average female college graduate today earns less than a man with a high-school diploma. While the media depicts working women as fast-track superwomen who have it all, the sad reality is that nearly three quarters of all female workers still earn less than $20,000 a year.[4]

## The Changing Workplace

The demographics of the workforce and the nature of work are changing rapidly. Historically, the typical American worker has been a white man with a high-school education employed in a manufacturing job. Today the workforce is becoming older, less educated, more ethnically diverse, and more female. At the same time our economy is shifting from manufacturing to service jobs. The level of literacy and basic skills of entry-level workers is dropping while the level of skill needed to perform well is increasing.[5]

Women and minorities will make up more than two thirds of the new workers in the next decade.[6] One of the biggest changes in the workforce is the increase in the numbers of women with young children. Fifty-four percent of married women whose youngest children are under six are in the labor force now, compared with 30 percent in 1970.[7] Seventy-one percent of the mothers in two-parent families with school-age children work.

Mergers and acquisitions, failures and downsizing, the expanding service sector and the globalization of American business are contributing to a flattening of hierarchies. There are fewer young people to enter the job market, and the average age of the workforce is getting older.[8] The aging of the workforce along with the changes in the structure of corporations means fewer management opportunities. In 1987, one worker in twenty was promoted to top management; in 2001, the ratio will be one in fifty.[9]

## Adapting to Change

The world is changing and the workplace of the future will have to change with it. In order to prosper, both employers and employees must adapt. The hierarchical, competitive male model is not the only way to do business. Many corporations are turning to new paradigms for doing business and finding them more efficient and effective.

The popularity of the concept of "reengineering" described in Michael Hammer and James Champy's best-selling book *Reengineering the Corporation*[10] is evidence that business is recognizing the need for change. Management gurus Hammer and Champy say that businesses that want to be successful in the twenty-first century will have to completely change their way of doing business. Companies must become organized around processes, not tasks and goals. Businesses will have to be more flexible to develop ways to individualize their delivery of goods and services to each client. Many businesses are experimenting with reducing the number of managers and developing self-managed work groups. Even IBM, the epitome of the hierarchical, conservative company, is now becoming more decentralized and stressing cooperation and the empowerment of individual workers.[11]

Progress is slow, but we are beginning to see a shift in the cultures of organizations. Workers no longer expect to spend whole careers at one corporation. The average American has held eight jobs by his or her fortieth birthday.[12] So corporations need new ways to keep workers invested and productive. Companies are moving toward open, cooperative structures. Employees, both men and women, want autonomy, self-development, and balance between work and family life. Benefits such as flexible work schedules, child-care assistance, and maternity and paternity leave are becoming essential for attracting and keeping good employees. The growth of computerization and telecommunications has made flex-time, part-time work, working from home, and job sharing valid and efficient ways to do business.

## Business Needs Women

There are as many management styles as there are managers. Every study of management style shows overlap in male and female styles, but there are some differences. Judy Rosener, a professor at the University of California, Irvine, compared the leadership styles of 230 members of the International Women's Forum with their male counterparts.[13] She found that male managers manage by using the power conferred by the organization. They think in terms of "transactions," offering rewards or trades for services rendered. Women concentrate on persuading subordinates to align their self-interest with the broader interests of the group. They do this by encouraging participation, and using charisma and personal contacts, rather than status, as their power base. Generally women are less interested in power than men are and more motivated by the desire to do a good job.

Businesses need women. The shrinking of the workforce means businesses won't be able to compete without the skills women have to offer. Women also bring a management style in tune with the new needs of corporations. The newest management books urge supervisors to include workers' ideas in decision making and foster cooperation. To increase efficiency, today's businesses are trimming inventories and striving to manufacture and deliver goods or services precisely when they are needed. Corporations are demanding that their managers develop the skills necessary to achieve these goals: empathy, understanding, caring, and attention to detail. This management style is comfortable and natural for many women.

Men are beginning to notice. In a 1993 *Management Today* article, Tom Lester informs us that there is a "growing acceptance that women's management abilities are valuable resources that no society or business can afford to ignore."[14]

## Don't Lose Yourself

In this book, I have been encouraging you to learn the rules of the game to help you better maneuver in the workplace as it is and to understand the men with whom you work. Learn the rules and use them to your benefit. But I don't want that message to overpower this one: *Value your strengths, stay true to yourself, and don't buy into a system that needs changing.*

Listen to your "women's intuition." Consider your feelings as well as your intellect when making decisions. Don't get caught in the trap of trying to imitate a "logical man." Intuition is based on unconscious knowledge, knowledge that is invaluable but impossible to verbalize. The unconscious has its own kind of logic. Act on it, trust it, but don't try to explain it. Just because it is illogical in male terms does not mean it is wrong. In fact, it is usually right.

Traditional male morality is a morality of individual rights. Traditional female morality is an ethic of responsibility. The problem with male morality is that it focuses on solutions and ignores how these solutions affect people. The problem with female morality is that it leads to taking care of everyone at one's own expense. Let's strive for a synthesis of the two, a morality that balances everyone's individual rights, *including one's own*, with an attempt not to hurt anyone. With this synthesis, women could be more comfortable with getting their needs met and men could become more responsive to the needs of others.

Don't smother your understanding and feelings for people and relationships. Find a way to use it to your advantage. The marketplace is by definition a competitive place, and there is a healthy side to competition. It inspires everyone to do their best. But so does cooperation. Cooperation and competition do not have to be mutually exclusive. There is a place for each.

## Through the Glass Ceiling

Change is a slow process and the present is far from perfect. Prejudice against women and minorities is alive and flourishing. In 1992, Congress and the Bush administration appointed a bipartisan board made up of lawmakers, corporate executives, and representatives of public-interest groups to study the progress women and minorities have made in business. This Glass Ceiling Commission issued its report on March 16, 1995. The report called progress made by women and minorities to shatter the glass ceiling "disappointingly slow."[15] "Before one can even look at the glass ceiling, one must get through the front door and into the building," the report said. "The fact is large numbers of minorities and women of all races and ethnicities are nowhere near the front door of Corporate America."

For me, the most disheartening finding of all was, "The overwhelming majority of CEOs interviewed . . . think of the glass ceiling as something that used to affect women—white and nonwhite—but that is no longer a real problem for them."[16] Senate Republican leader Robert Dole pushed for the creation of the commission as part of the Civil Rights Act of 1991. He is now calling for a reassessment of affirmative action.

Women have certainly made inroads in business. The momentum is in the right direction, but I am concerned it will not continue. Without ongoing change, the workplace will persist in depriving women and minorities of the same opportunities that white males have. Clinton administration officials do not expect the Republican-controlled Congress to carry out the Glass Ceiling Commission's recommendations for government action.[17] And this should not be acceptable to us.

As part of Rule 2: Act strong, I suggested women remember this maxim: It is inexcusable not to try to remedy any situation you do not like. If you don't like something your government is doing—or not doing—speak up. Pay attention to what your legislators are doing and let them know how you feel about issues that affect you.

## Women on the Board

The irony of sexism is that companies need women, especially in the boardroom. Women on boards have both a symbolic and a direct effect on a business's bottom line. In a world populated by female employees, customers, and stockholders, diversity is good PR and, it follows, good business. Companies hurt themselves by excluding or not promoting qualified women. Susan King, a senior VP at Corning:

> A question you would ask about a company that still has an all-white, all-male board is: Is this company in tune

with the times? It's a real indication of where they think they are in the market.[18]

Covenant Investment Management rated one thousand of the country's largest companies on their records in hiring and advancing women and compared it with their stock performance during 1988 to 1992. Companies that ranked in the top 20 percent in terms of advancing female employees outperformed the market by 2.5 percent; companies found in the bottom 20 percent were outpaced by 8 percent.[19]

The impact Jill Ker Conway, a former Smith College president, had on Nike when she joined its board is a good example of the benefits women directors bring. When Ms. Conway joined the board in 1987, Nike did not see women as a distinct market. Women's products were, essentially, male products colored pink. From her position on the board, she convinced Nike that they needed a women's division, run by women, focused exclusively on selling to women. Her strategic insights led to the creation of a women's division in 1990. This division now accounts for 20 percent of Nike's domestic revenues.

Women on boards not only benefit the company, they benefit other women. Ms. Conway says, "On every board on which I'm active, I try to work in terms of the needs of families."[20] Nike included a day-care facility when they planned their new headquarters. In a Catalyst survey of Fortune 1000 companies, 64 percent of the female board members polled said it was their responsibility to push for affirmative action. Fifty-nine percent said it was their duty to suggest additional women to serve on boards, and 52 percent said it was their job to address work/family policies.[21]

Many men believe that there are so few women on boards because there are few women qualified to sit on boards. This is simply not true. Catalyst asked forty-six CEOs to estimate the number of qualified women board candidates in the United

States. Almost half said 250 or less. This number is a glaring underestimation. There are already five hundred women sitting on Fortune 1000 boards.[22] Although there are few women heading large corporations, there are hundreds of senior female executives, CEOs of smaller companies, former government agency heads, and heads of nonprofit organizations who would make excellent board members. Corollary 2 of Rule 5—Make yourself visible—is particularly apt here. Zoe Baird, who is Aetna's general counsel, wasn't invited to join any Fortune 1000 boards until after the Nannygate debacle. She simply wasn't noticed.

Learning the rules of the game is only the *beginning*. Right now these rules are the rules business plays by—but it doesn't have to continue this way. As more women enter the workplace and as more women reach higher positions, there is an enormous potential for change. The culture of the workplace of the future can, and should, be a culture that values people, cares about the quality of life, is responsive to family needs—and is more efficient and effective than ever before. Let's work together to make it happen.

# Rules for the Game of "Work"

### RULE 1: ACT COMPETENT

1. Act like you know what you're doing, even if you're not sure that you do know.
2. Ask for help only when you really need it.
3. Brag about your accomplishments and flaunt your talents.
4. Don't advertise your mistakes.

### RULE 2: ACT STRONG

1. Always try to take control and be in control.
2. Do not be obviously dependent on a superior.
3. Do not let your opponent know he has "gotten to you," even if he has.
4. Do not sulk or complain if things do not go your way.
5. Act like the competent professional you are, not the stereotype of a businesswoman.

### Rule 3: Keep Playing to Win Even When the Game Is No Longer Fun

1. Long hours may be part of the job.
2. Getting clients or generating business can be as much a part of the job as the job.
3. There may be times when it is best to stretch the truth or to lie.

### Rule 4: Don't Get Emotionally Involved While Playing the Game

1. Don't take comments made by opponents or colleagues personally.
2. Don't become too attached to your clients or your goals.
3. Only show anger at appropriate times.

### Rule 5: Being Aggressive Is Part of the Game

1. Choose the team you want to play on and work to be picked for that team.
2. Make yourself visible.
3. Ask for interesting work.
4. Take risks.

### Rule 6: Fighting Is Part of the Game

1. Fight fair.
2. Don't be too passive or too aggressive.
3. Find your opponent's Achilles' heel and go for it.
4. Know when to stop.
5. Let your opponent save face.
6. Be a gracious winner and a good loser.

## Rule 7: You Are Part of a Team

1. Teams wear uniforms.
2. Teammates help each other.
3. Always be loyal to your team.
4. The good of your team comes before your personal interests.
5. Always give 100 percent ... or make it look like you do.

# ENDNOTES

## Chapter One

1. Carol Nagy Jacklin, "Female and Male: Issues of Gender," *American Psychologist* 44: 2 (1989), 127–133.

2. Nancy Chodorow, *Feminism and Psychoanalytic Theory* (New Haven, CT: Yale University Press, 1989).

3. Christopher Leone and Kevin Robertson, "Some Effects of Sex-linked Clothing and Gender Schema on the Stereotyping of Infants," *Journal of Social Psychology* 129:5 (1989), 609–619.

4. Judith V. Jordan, Alexandra G. Kaplan, Jean Baker Miller, Irene P. Stiver, and Janet L. Surrey, eds., *Women's Growth in Connection: Writings from the Stone Center* (New York: The Guilford Press, 1991).

5. Janet L. Surrey, "The 'Self-in-Relation': A Theory of Women's Development," in Judith V. Jordan, et al., *Women's Growth in Connection: Writings from the Stone Center*, 51–66.

6. Karen Horney, "The Dread of Women," *International Journal of Psychoanalysis* 13 (1932).

## Chapter Two

1. George Herbert Mead, *Mind, Self and Society* (Chicago: University of Chicago Press, 1934).

2. Eleanor Maccoby and Carol Nagy Jacklin, *The Psychology of Sex Differences* (Stanford: Stanford University Press, 1974).

3. Janet Lever, "Sex Differences in the Games Children Play," *Social Prob-*

*lems* 23 (1976), 478–483, and "Sex Differences in the Complexity of Children's Play and Games," *American Sociological Review* 43 (1978), 471–483.

4. S. Colby, L. Kohlberg, J. Gills, and M. Lerberman, "A Longitudinal Study of Moral Judgment," *Monographs of the Society for Research in Child Development* 48 (1983), 1–96.

5. Daniel N. Maltz and Ruth A. Borker, "A Cultural Approach to Male-Female Miscommunication," in John J. Bumperez, ed., *Language and Social Identity* (Cambridge: Cambridge University Press, 1982), 196–216. Also see Eleanor E. Maccoby, "Gender and Relationships: A Developmental Account," *American Psychologist* 45:4 (1990), 513–520.

6. Eleanor E. Maccoby, "Gender and Relationships: A Developmental Account."

## Chapter Three

1. A. Pazy, "The Persistence of Pro-male Bias Despite Identical Information Regarding Causes of Success," *Organizational Behavior and Human Decision Processes* 38 (1986), 243–256.

2. William Grimes, "Night of the Long Knives," *New York Times Magazine*, April 28, 1991, 69.

## Chapter Four

1. Lyn Mikel Brown and Carol Gilligan, *Meeting at the Crossroads: Women's Psychology and Girls' Development* (New York: Ballantine Books, 1993).

## Chapter Six

1. Arlie Hochschild with Anne Machung, *The Second Shift: Working Parents and the Revolution at Home* (New York: Viking, 1989).

## Chapter Nine

1. Daniel Pearl, "Sky Warriors Take Would-be Flyboys on Flights of Fancy," *The Wall Street Journal*, August 28, 1991, A1.

## Chapter Ten

1. Sandra Forsythe, Mary F. Drake, and Charles E. Cox, "Influence of Applicant's Dress on Interviewer's Selection Decisions," *Journal of Applied Psychology* 70:2 (1985), 374–378.

## Chapter Twelve

1. American Association of University Women, *How Schools Shortchange Girls* (Washington, DC: AAUW Educational Foundation and National Education Association, 1992).

2. Irene P. Stiver, "Work Inhibitions in Women," in Judith V. Jordan, et al., *Women's Growth in Connection: Writings from the Stone Center*, 223–236.

3. B. Weiner, I. Frieze, A. Kukla, L. Reed, S. Rest, and R. M. Rosenbaum, *Perceiving the Causes of Success and Failure* (Morristown, NJ: General Learning Press, 1971), and Julian Rotter, "Generalized Expectancies for Internal Versus External Control of Reinforcement," *Psychological Monographs* 80:1 (1966).

4. V. J. Crandall, W. Katkovsky, and A. Preston, "Motivational and Ability Determinants of Young Children's Intellectual Achievement Behaviors," *Child Development* 33:3 (1962), 643–661.

5. A. T. Beck, "Cognition, Affect, and Psychopathology," *Archives of General Psychiatry* 24 (1971), 495–500, and A. T. Beck, *Cognitive Therapy and the Emotional Disorders* (New York: International Universities Press, 1976).

## Chapter Thirteen

1. T. J. D'Zurilla and M. R. Goldfried, "Problem Solving and Behavior Modification," *Journal of Abnormal Psychology* 78 (1971), 107–126. Also see M. R. Goldfried, "Psychotherapy as Coping Skills Training," in M. J. Mahoney, ed., *Psychotherapy Process: Current Issues and Future Directions* (New York: Plenum, 1980) and T. J. D'Zurilla, *Problem-Solving Therapy: A Social Competence Approach to Clinical Intervention* (New York: Springer, 1986).

## Introduction to Part Four

1. Margaret Mead, *Male and Female* (New York: William Morrow, 1949), 303.

## Chapter Fifteen

1. Bill Watterson, *Calvin and Hobbes*, distributed by Universal Press Syndicate, *Sunday Inquirer*, March 11, 1990.

2. Greg Logan, "NFL Supports Olson vs. Pats; Club Must Pay $50,000; 3 Fined a Total of $22,500; the Olson Controversy," *Newsday*, November 28, 1990, 163.

3. Michael Dobbs, "Social Climate Changes but Finns Still Hot for Sauna," *Philadelphia Inquirer*, March 8, 1992, A11.

## Chapter Seventeen

1. Arthur J. Lange and Patricia Jakubowski, *Responsible Assertive Behavior: Cognitive/Behavioral Procedures for Trainers* (Champaign, IL: Research Press, 1976), 18; and Elaina Zuker, *Mastering Assertiveness Skills: Power and Positive Influence at Work* (New York: AMACOM, 1983).

## Chapter Eighteen

1. M. P. Koss, "Changed Lives: The Psychological Impact of Sexual Harassment," Michele A. Paludi, ed., *Ivory Power: Sexual Harassment on Campus* (Albany: State University of New York Press, 1990).

2. D. G. Kilpatrick, "Treatment and Counseling Needs of Women Veterans Who Were Raped, Otherwise Sexually Assaulted, or Sexually Harassed During Military Service," testimony before the Senate Committee on Veterans' Affairs, June 30, 1992.

3. E. G. Collins and C. Blodgett, "Sexual Harassment: Some See It . . . Some Don't," *Harvard Business Review* 59 (1981), 76–95.

4. E. Bravo and E. Cassedy, *The 9 to 5 Guide to Combating Sexual Harassment* (New York: John Wiley and Sons, 1992).

5. Dale Moss, "Just as Vulnerable," *The Pennsylvania Lawyer*, Pennsylvania Bar Association, March 1992, 8–10.

6. American Psychiatric Association, "Sexual Harassment Can Lead to Psychiatric Dysfunction," *Psychiatric News*, April 6, 1990, 18.

7. Louise F. Fitzgerald and Alayne J. Ormerod, "Perceptions of Sexual Harassment: The Influence of Gender and Academic Context," *Psychology of Women Quarterly* 15 (1991), 281–294.

8. P. Crull, "Stress Effects of Sexual Harassment on the Job: Implications for Counseling," *American Journal of Orthopsychiatry* 52 (1982), 539–544. Also see M. Junger, "Women's Experiences of Sexual Harassment," *British Journal of Criminology* 27 (1987), 358–383, and J. E. Gruber and L. Bjorn, "Women's Responses to Sexual Harassment: Analysis of Sociocultural, Organizational, and Personal Resource Models," *Social Science Quarterly* 67 (1986), 814–826.

9. Ibid.

10. P. Crull, "Sexual Harassment and Women's Health," in W. Chavkin, ed., *Double Exposure* (New York: Monthly Review Press, 1984). Also see J. Hamilton and J. Dokart, "Working Paper on Legal Reform in the Area of Sexual Harassment: Contributions from Social Science," paper presented at the First National Conference to Promote Men and Women Working Productively Together, Bellevue, WA, March 1992, and J. Dokart, "Working Paper on Legal Reform in the Area of Sexual Harassment: Procedural and Evidentiary Reform," paper presented at the First National Conference on Sex and Power Issues in the Workplace, Bellevue, WA, March 1992.

## Chapter Nineteen

1. Susan E. Tifft, "Board Gains: Women Start to Win a Place at the Table," *Working Woman*, 19:2 (1994), 36.

2. Elizabeth E. Janice, "The Male-Female Wage Gap," *1995 Information Please Business Almanac and Source* (Boston: Houghton Mifflin Co., 1994).

3. Frank Swoboda, " 'Glass Ceiling' Firmly in Place; Panel Finds Minorities, Women Are Rare in Management," *The Washington Post*, March 16, 1995, A01.

4. Elizabeth E. Janice, "The Male-Female Wage Gap."

5. Lynn R. Offermann and Marilyn K. Gowing, "Organizations of the Future: Changes and Challenges," *American Psychologist* 45:2 (1990) 95–108.

6. Ibid.

7. C. D. Foster, M. A. Siegel, and N. R. Jacobs, eds., *Women's Changing Roles* (Wylie, TX: Information Aids, 1988).

8. Lynn R. Offermann and Marilyn K. Gowing, "Organizations of the Future."

9. E. C. Arnett, "Futurists Gaze into Business's Crystal Ball," *The Washington Post*, July 20, 1989, F1–F2.

10. Michael Hammer and James Champy, *Reengineering the Corporation: A Manifesto for Business Revolution* (New York: HarperCollins Publishers, 1993).

11. Tom Lester, "A Woman's Place . . . (in Management)," *Management Today* 5 (1993), 46.

12. Runzheimer International, "Jobs Held by Race, Sex and Age," *1995 Information Please Business Almanac and Source* (Boston: Houghton Mifflin Co., 1994).

13. Judy B. Rosener, "Ways Women Lead," *Harvard Business Review* 120 (1990), 301.

14. Tom Lester, "A Woman's Place . . . (in Management)."

15. Frank Swoboda, " 'Glass Ceiling' Firmly in Place."

16. Ibid.

17. Ibid.

18. Susan E. Tifft, "Board Gains."

19. Ibid.

20. Ibid.

21. Ibid.

22. Ibid.

# SELECTED REFERENCES

Alberti, Robert E., and Emmons, Michael L. 1990. *Your Perfect Right: A Guide to Assertive Living.* San Luis Obispo, CA: Impact Publishers.

Bargad, Adena, and Hyde, Janet Shibley. 1991. "Women's Studies: A Study of Feminist Identity Development in Women." *Psychology of Women Quarterly* 15:2, 181–202.

Beck, A. T. 1976. *Cognitive Therapy and the Emotional Disorders.* New York: International Universities Press.

———. 1988. *Love Is Never Enough.* New York: Harper and Row.

Belenky, M. F., Clinchy, B. M., Goldberger, N. R., and Tarule, J. M. 1986. *Women's Ways of Knowing.* New York: Basic Books.

Bepko, Claudia, and Krestan, Jo-Ann. 1990. *Too Good for Her Own Good: Breaking Free from the Burden of Female Responsibility.* New York: Harper and Row.

Bernard, Jessie. 1988. "The Inferiority Curriculum." *Psychology of Women Quarterly* 12:3, 261–68.

Bravo, Ellen, and Cassedy, Ellen. 1992. *The 9 to 5 Guide to Combating Sexual Harassment: Candid Advice from the National Association of Working Women.* New York: John Wiley and Sons.

Brown, Lyn Mikel, and Gilligan, Carol. 1993. *Meeting at the Crossroads: Women's Psychology and Girls' Development.* New York: Ballantine Books.

Burley-Allen, M. 1983. *Managing Assertively.* New York: John Wiley and Sons.

Cantor, Dorothy W., and Bernay, Toni, with Stoess, Jean. 1992. *Women in Power: The Secrets of Leadership.* Boston: Houghton Mifflin.

Chodorow, Nancy. 1974. "Family Structure and Feminine Personality." *Woman, Culture and Society.* Ed. by M. Z. Rosaldo and L. Lamphere. Stanford: Stanford University Press.

———. 1978. *The Reproduction of Mothering.* Berkeley: University of California Press.

Denmark, Florence L. 1993. "Women, Leadership, and Empowerment." *Psychology of Women Quarterly* 17: 3, 343–56.

Dobson, Keith S., ed. 1988. *Handbook of Cognitive-Behavioral Therapies.* New York: The Guilford Press.

Elgin, S. H. 1987. *The Last Word on the Gentle Art of Verbal Self-Defense.* New York: Prentice-Hall.

Eagly, Alice H., Mladinic, Antonio, and Otto, Stacey. 1991. "Are Women Evaluated More Favorably Than Men: An Analysis of Attitudes, Beliefs, and Emotions." *Psychology of Women Quarterly* 15:2, 203–16.

Ellis, A., and Harper, R. 1979. *A New Guide to Rational Living.* Englewood Cliffs, NJ: Prentice-Hall.

Fisher, R., and Ury, W. 1983. *Getting to Yes: Negotiating Agreement Without Giving In.* New York: Penguin Books.

Gilligan, Carol. 1982. *In a Different Voice.* Cambridge, MA: Harvard University Press.

Griscom, Joan L. 1992. "Women and Power: Definition, Dualism, and Difference." *Psychology of Women Quarterly* 16:4, 389–414.

Grossman, Hildreth Y., and Chester, Nia Lane, eds. 1990. *The Experience and Meaning of Work in Women's Lives.* Hillsdale, NJ: Erlbaum.

Hare-Mustin, Rachel T., and Marecek, Jeanne, eds. 1990. *Making a Difference: Psychology and the Construction of Gender.* New Haven, CT: Yale University Press.

Hartup, Willard W. 1989. "Social Relationships and Their Developmental Significance." *American Psychologist* 44:2, 120–26.

Hatcher, Maxine Arnold. 1991. "The Corporate Woman of the 1990s: Maverick or Innovator." *Psychology of Women Quarterly* 15:2, 251–60.

Hogan, Robert, Curphy, Gordon J., and Hogan, Joyce. 1994. "What We Know About Leadership: Effectiveness and Personality." *American Psychologist* 49:6, 493–504.

Hollander, Edwin P., and Offermann, Lynn R. 1990. "Power and Leadership in Organizations: Relationships in Transition." *American Psychologist* 45:2, 179–89.

Horner, Althea. 1989. *The Wish for Power and the Fear of Having It.* New York: Jason Aaronson.

Horney, Karen. 1939. *New Ways in Psychoanalysis.* New York: W. W. Norton & Co.

Jordan, Judith V., Kaplan, Alexandra G., Miller, Jean Baker, Stiver, Irene P., and Surrey, Janet L., eds. 1991. *Women's Growth in Connection: Writings from the Stone Center.* New York: The Guilford Press.

Kanter, Rosabeth Moss. 1977. *Men and Women of the Corporation.* New York: Basic Books.

Keen, Sam. 1991. *Fire in the Belly: On Being a Man.* New York: Bantam Books.

Kelley, Colleen. 1979. *Assertion Training: A Facilitator's Guide.* La Jolla, CA: University Associates.

Kimmel, Michael S. 1993. "In Question: What Do Men Want?" *Harvard Business Review* 71:6, 50.

LaFrance, Marianne. 1992. "Gender and Interruptions: Individual Infraction or Violation of the Social Order." *Psychology of Women Quarterly* 16:4, 497–512.

Lever, Janet. 1978. "Sex Differences in the Complexity of Children's Play and Games." *American Sociological Review* 43, 471–83.

Levinson, Harry. 1994. "Why the Behemoths Fell: Psychological Roots of Corporate Failure." *American Psychologist* 49:5, 428–36.

Lorber, Judith, and Farrell, Susan A., eds. 1991. *The Social Construction of Gender.* Newbury Park, CA: Sage.

Maccoby, Eleanor, and Jacklin, Carol. 1974. *The Psychology of Sex Differences.* Stanford: Stanford University Press.

Matthews, Karen A., and Rodin, Judith. 1989. "Women's Changing Work Roles: Impact on Health, Family and Public Policy." *American Psychologist* 44:11, 1389–93.

Mead, George Herbert. 1934. *Mind, Self and Society.* Chicago: University of Chicago Press.

Miller, Cynthia L., and Cummins, A. Gaye. 1992. "An Examination of Women's Perspectives on Power." *Psychology of Women Quarterly* 16:4, 415–28.

Miller, Jean Baker. 1976. *Toward a New Psychology of Women.* Boston: Beacon Press.

Morrison, Ann M., and Glinow, Mary Ann. 1990. "Women and Minorities in Management." *American Psychologist* 45:2, 200–08.

Offermann, Lynn R., and Beil, Cheryl. 1992. "Achievement Styles of Women Leaders and Their Peers: Toward an Understanding of Women and Leadership." *Psychology of Women Quarterly* 16:1, 37–56.

Paludi, Michele A., ed. 1990. *Ivory Power: Sexual Harassment on Campus.* Albany: State University of New York Press.

Phelps, S. 1987. *The Assertive Woman.* San Luis Obispo, CA: Impact Publishers.

Piaget, Jean. 1965. *The Moral Judgement of the Child* (1932). New York: The Free Press.

Plomin, Robert. 1989. "Environment and Genes: Determinants of Behavior." *American Psychologist* 44:2, 105–11.

Rogoff, Barbara, and Morelli, Gilda. 1989. "Perspectives on Children's Development from Cultural Psychology." *American Psychologist* 44:2, 343–48.

Rotter, Julian. 1966. "Generalized Expectancies for Internal Versus External Control of Reinforcement." *Psychological Monographs* 80:1.

Scarr, Sandra, Phillips, Deborah, and McCartney, Kathleen. 1989. "Working Mothers and Their Families." *American Psychologist* 44:11, 1402–09.

Schein, Edgar H. 1990. "Organizational Culture." *American Psychologist* 45:2, 109–19.

Seligman, Martin E. P. 1991. *Learned Optimism.* New York: Alfred A. Knopf.

Serbin, L. A., Sprafkin, C., Elman, M., and Doyle, A. 1984. "The Early Development of Sex Differentiated Patterns of Social Influence." *Canadian Journal of Social Science* 14, 923–35.

Stoller, Robert J. 1964. "A Contribution to the Study of Gender Identity." *International Journal of Psycho-analysis* 45, 220–26.

Stratham, Anne. 1987. "The Gender Model Visited: Differences in the Management Styles of Men and Women." *Sex Roles* 16:7, 409–27.

Tannen, Deborah. 1990. *You Just Don't Understand: Men and Women in Conversation.* New York: William Morrow.

———. 1994. *Talking From 9 to 5: How Women's and Men's Conversational Styles Affect Who Gets Heard, Who Gets Credit and What Gets Done at Work.* New York: William Morrow.

Voydanoff, Patricia. 1988. "Women, Work, and Family: Bernard's Perspective on the Past, Present, and Future." *Psychology of Women Quarterly* 12:3, 269–80.

Weiss, Robert S. 1990. *Staying the Course: The Emotional and Social Lives of Men Who Do Well at Work.* New York: The Free Press.

Yoder, Janice D., and Kahn, Arnold S. 1992. "Toward a Feminist Understanding of Women and Power." *Psychology of Women Quarterly* 16:4, 381–88.

# ABOUT THE AUTHOR

ADRIENNE MENDELL is a licensed psychologist in private practice in Philadelphia specializing in gender issues in the workplace. Her popular workshops, seminars, and small group programs have helped hundreds of women surmount barriers and reach their career potential. She is an avid sailor and teaches sailing as a volunteer for the U.S. Coast Guard Auxiliary.